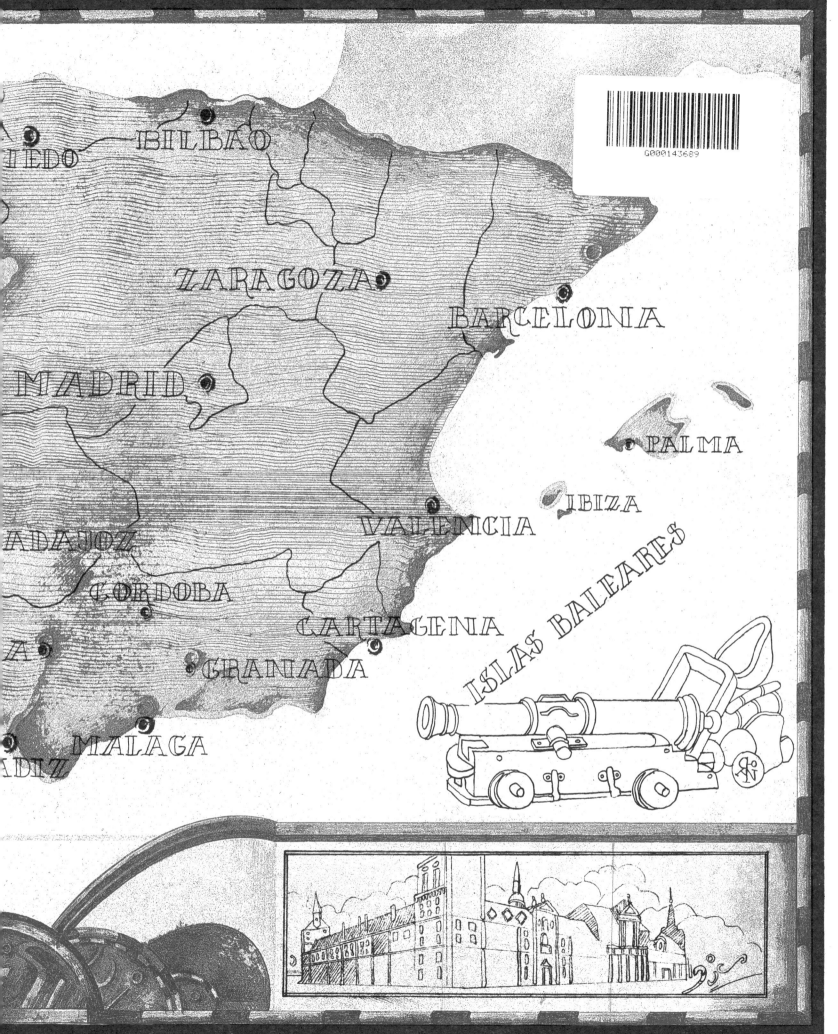

SPAIN

FLINT RIVER

1990

A Motovun Group Book

© World copyright 1990
FLINT RIVER PRESS Ltd., London

First published in the United Kingdom
by Flint River Press Ltd.
26 Litchfield Street
London WC2H 9NJ

Distribuited by
Philip Wilson Publishers Ltd.
26 Litchfield Street
London WC2H 9NJ

ISBN: 1-871489-06-7

Photographs by
INCAFO Picture Library, Madrid:
Teresa Alonso
Jorge Blassi
Antonio Camoyán
Alberto Carafato
Juan Fernandez
Candy Lopesino
Carlos Zapata

Werner Forman Archive, London

Robert Harding Picture Library,
London

Christine Pinheira, Paris

Editor
Madge Phillips

End-paper design
Zoran Mujebegović

Color separation by
Summerfield Press, Florence

Printed and bound in Italy by
Nova Zincografica Fiorentina,
Florence, 1990

CONTENTS

ESPAÑA

SPAIN

Text by

DENNIS GUNTON

Originated and developed by

NEBOJŠA BATO TOMAŠEVIĆ

Designed by

GANE ALEKSIĆ

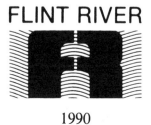

FLINT RIVER

1990

Introduction

A Personal View

Spain has always seemed separate from the rest of Europe and, indeed, from the rest of the world, despite having played such an outstanding role in discovery, conquest and colonisation. In the seventeenth century, it has to be remembered, her possessions in Europe alone stretched from Brussels in the north to Sicily and Gibraltar in the south. Communications between provinces were maintained by tenuous overland routes while the Spanish sea lanes were in the hands of as powerful a maritime power as the world had ever seen.

Away across the Atlantic, Spanish America was most of the New World until well into the nineteenth century; it was (or had been) the whole of South America except for Brazil, and all of Central America, including Mexico. The Spanish flag fluttered over extensive areas of North America, too: California, Florida and Louisiana, the last acquired from France in 1762, but retroceded under French pressure in 1800. Napoleon, recognising the liability the territory would present in a war with Great Britain, then decided to cede Louisiana to the United States. In 1803 the treaty was ratified and the U.S. flag raised over New Orleans on December 20. As the Spanish empire crumbled in the early nineteenth century, Florida was relinquished to the United States in 1821, and a year later California gave its allegiance to newly-independent Mexico.

After a dazzling flush of achievement Spain, which had seemed invincible, unrivaled in her knowledge of the New World with all its rich sources of wealth, ceased to be an imperial power.

Even the snow-capped barrier of the Pyrenees was no safeguard against the effects of the French Revolution, when Napoleon not only occupied Spain and set his brother Joseph on the throne, but helped to implant ideas of liberty, equality, unity and most importantly — self-government among the peoples of the Spanish colonies.

The most distinctive remnants left by the age when Spain was the greatest civilisation on earth are the sonorous names of locations all over the world and the dispersed usage of the elegant Spanish language, a language of the Romance group and itself a subject of contention in the country of origin.

The reason why Spain was so often a victim of outside influences was the lack of unity at home, where there were persistent conflicts between landowners and workers, between central authority and the regions, traditionalists and reformers. It may have been the nationally exhausting repercussions of the French Revolution that left Spain too debilitated to notice the advent of the other great radical change of the era, and to benefit no more than it did from the Industrial Revolution.

If the burden of Spain's past is to some extent the legacy of neglect, it is all the more remarkable to witness the spectacular transformation of the last few decades. Anyone visiting Spain, as I did for the first time, in the late Fifties found their pleasure diminished because the people themselves found so little to relish. To the foreigners from a Europe recovering from World War II, the Civil War seemed so much further away; the sunshine should have had less shadow and it was disturbing to see that there was so little pleasure in the past or confidence in the future.

How different are things today, although not all the advances have been achieved without growing pains. True, there has been inflation — as there has been in other parts of Europe; unemployment — inevitable as a neglected agriculture mechanises; isolated acts of terrorism — but the political options reduce the need for military solutions; increased crime — by no means confined to Spain, any more than Spain is alone in having problems with drugs, housing, education, social change and the family. What is unmistakable, however, is the vitality, the confidence and the expectations which have burst to the surface. It is at least possible that more Spaniards enjoy Spain now than at any time in the past, and they are outnumbered by the tourists who come in ever growing numbers, year after year. Moreover, the recent achievements of Spaniards in the fields of international sport and entertainment indicate not only talent, but more leisure time and wider opportunities for recreation, in the past mostly confined to peninsular forms of gratification such as bullfighting and fiestas.

More important than the absence of Spain from global arenas of sport and entertainment has been the want of a national voice — in the broadest cultural sense — for a very long time, arguably for most of this century. It is probable that, as a result, more foreigners have read about Spain from the pens of Hemingway, Michener, Orwell or V.S. Pritchett than they have from Spanish creative writers translated into English. From 1945-1984, some 700 novels with Spain as a setting were published in the United Kingdom. Apart from a few titles translated from the Spanish, which include Cervantes' 'Don Quixote' and V.B. Ibáñez' 'Blood and Sand', the overwhelming majority are written by foreigners, for example: L. Feuchtanger's 'Rachel Jewess of Toledo', G. Greene's 'Monsieur Quixote', S. Shellaberger's 'Captain from Castile' and F.P. Keyes' 'Letter from Spain'.

The case of Vicente Blasco Ibáñez illustrates the power of Hollywood — towards which so many countries have had to look for an internationally marketable version of their culture. A Republican and radical writer, Ibáñez spent most of his life exiled from Spain. His sensational novel of the first world war, 'Four Horsemen of the Apocalypse' (1916), made him internationally famous; the film version (1921), which owed a good deal to expert script-writers and a legendary star, Rudolph Valentino, was a huge artistic and financial success. In 1922 Valentino starred in 'Blood and Sand', another money-spinning triumph for the actor, Paramount Studios and the author of the story, in which a handsome matador falls under the spell of a wealthy aristocratic 'femme fatale'. A successful remake in 1941 brought international stardom to Rita Hayworth in the female lead. Although the films owed more to expert adaption and the Hollywood stars than to the intrinsic quality of the novels, now very dated, Blasco Ibáñez is one of the very few Spanish writers to have caught the popular imagination abroad.

If Spain has not found authentic voices or writers able to appeal to the world at large, it is not surprising that so many fanciful interpretations of Spain have come from other sources. Among the most ludicrous was a whole genre of films, swashbucklers, which featured heavily laden Spanish galleons on the Spanish Main, their holds crammed with the gem-studded gold of the Indies, their passenger list invariably including captured, yet sumptuously costumed, ladies of rank. Crewed by knaves and captained by dons as infamous as they were incompetent, the galleons were invariably captured by handsome, athletic, freedom-loving sons-of-the-sea, who, on the whole, spoke with an American accent. The model had little by way of historical truth, although it presented one of the most widely circulated images of imperial Spain at the height of its military prowess.

More seriously there is the example of 'For Whom the Bell Tolls' by Ernest Hemingway, a novel, and later a film, which survives as one of the most popular imaginative accounts of the issues at stake in the Civil War. Where, we may ask, are the comparable Spanish versions of this bitter and bloody conflict? The answer may lie in the detectable thread of secrecy running through Spanish history, an understandable preference not to be laughed at and, when losing, an inability to learn enough from how the loss came about.

Some of the most profound insights into the Civil War came from a foreigner writing in Spanish — the Chilean poet Pablo Neruda, who won the Nobel prize in 1971 and died in 1973. In 1934, aged thirty, he was assigned to a diplomatic post in Madrid, where his communist beliefs led him to clash with fascist groups and to his eventual withdrawal to Santiago (a city named after the patron

saint of Spain) in 1937. A collection of his poems, 'Spain in our Hearts' (España en el Corazon), includes titles which leave no doubt about his allegiance: 'Spain, poor through the fault of the rich'; 'Madrid'; 'Song for the mothers of the slain militiamen'; 'Battle of the Jarama River' and many others which convey with eloquence and pain his commitment in the conflict. Two Nobel Prize winners, Hemingway and Neruda, took up the Republican cause. One wrote prose in English, the other wrote poetry in Spanish; both took the losers' side, rarely the best means of gaining a hearing. There may be a clue to the Spanish silence in Neruda's 'I explain a few things', when he writes:

> "Federico, do you remember
> under the ground,
> do you remember my house with balconies where
> June light smothered flowers in your mouth?"

The Federico in the poem is Federico García Lorca, poet, dramatist, lecturer, folklorist, musician, director of a theatrical group — a prodigious talent — who was executed in Granada, aged thirty-seven, at the outbreak of the war. If Spain's voice seems too often silent, the reason is not always complex.

An elderly foreign commentator, in the fourteenth century, was Geoffrey Chaucer. In the 'Canterbury Tales' he makes an amusing reference to Spanish wine which, given the enormous and growing popularity of such wine today, suggests the pilgrims to and from Santiago de Compostella may have acquired a taste for the fortified wines from the south and encouraged their importation into England.

> "Keep clear of wine, I tell you, white or red,
> Especially Spanish wines which they provide
> And have on sale in Fish Street and Cheapside.
> That wine mysteriously finds its way
> To mix itself with others — shall we say
> Spontaneously? — that grow in other regions.
> So when a man has had a drink or two
> Though he may think he is at home with you
> In Cheapside, I assure you he is in Spain
> Where it was made, at Lepé I maintain,
> Not even at Bordeaux."

Dwellers in Cheapside, a mercantile area of London, were familiar with the fermented juice of grapes: it is recorded that the water conduits there ran with wine to celebrate the birth of the Black Prince, eldest son of Edward III. Not only did the prince later maintain a brilliant court in Bordeaux, he allied his forces to those of Peter I (Pedro the Cruel) of Castile and León when helping to restore him to his throne. Lepé, an ancient castled town near the southern border with Portugal, long famous for good wine and figs, is now one of the most prosperous areas in Spain, from which 40,000 tons of strawberries are exported annually to fellow European Community countries.

Loss of empire, economic stagnation and repressive government throughout much of the nineteenth and twentieth centuries were likely to dampen the spirit of any nation. It comes, therefore, as an agreeable surprise for a foreigner in Spain today, amidst all the mushrooming developments of modern motorways, football stadiums, holiday resorts, high-rise hotels, boutiques, discothèques and airports, to find that the Spaniard himself is generous, helpful and free of the distrust that a history of declining fortune might legitimately have fostered. A new Spain is clearly in the making, a modern Spain which has to include industrial estates and dormitory suburbs. Stretching from the Balearics to the Canaries, it contains neon-lit coasts dedicated to pleasure and leisure but still retaining the feel of wind, sun, glittering sea, cornfields and olive groves. More importantly, it has the Spaniards.

All the variety of Spain itself can be found in the people, who say of themselves: the Catalan saves, the Andalusian sings, the Valencian sighs, the Basque acts, the Castilian dreams, the Estremaduran fights and the Galician yearns for what cannot be. All of which may or may not have the truth that is suspect in most generalisations about national characteristics, but does not obscure the fact the people of Spain, whatever part they are from, can stake a special claim to an extraordinary flair for the art of living. At its most flamboyant it takes the form of the fiesta, at its most enduring it is the capacity to make the best of things. Somewhere in between is the ability to find enough time to eat, drink and talk, that most subtle yet effective expression of a people bristling with ideas, humor and enthusiasm.

Ferdinand, King of Spain, engraving
from the famous letter (printed in
Basel, 1494) sent by Christopher
Colombus to Sánchez from his first
voyage.

Land of Sunshine and Shadow

The Iberian Peninsula, comprising Spain and Portugal, is one of the three fingers extending from the southern underside of Europe into the Mediterranean. All three have been the motherland to vast empires in a chronological passage westward from Greece, through Rome to Iberia. It is widely believed that the Iberians, from whom the name Iberia (Land of Rivers) comes, arrived from Africa in the neolithic period and that a Celtic migration followed from the north much later. Certainly the Celts and Iberians merged, but the name of the Iberians survives, unlike some other names given to Spain in the past, among them Edetania and Hesperia. It is probable the Romans adopted the Phoenician word Hispania, said to mean 'island of rabbits': if true, it throws as much doubt upon the accuracy of Phoenician geographers as it does upon their flair for symbolic nomenclature. Bulls and eagles perhaps, rabbits definitely not.

Demarcation in Spain owes everything to physical geography and climate, powerfully influenced by two great seas: to the west the Atlantic and to the east the Mediterranean. One great natural barrier — the Pyrenees — straddles the northern ramparts studded with lonely valleys, walnut contours and snow-ridged peaks, while, by contrast, the southern borders taper away to the Straits of Gibraltar where only eight miles of salt water separate Africa and Europe, the Atlantic and the Mediterranean. Almost as important is the rugged nature of the land mass itself. Spain occupies 190,114 square miles of the Iberian Peninsula, an area less than France but twice the size of the British Isles or West Germany, and as big as California and South Carolina combined. A large portion of the country, some forty percent, is a plateau of inhospitable winds and sparsely populated steppe — *meseta* — which extends from the Cantabrian Mountains in the north to the Sierra Morena in the south, and from the Portuguese border in the west to the low valleys that fringe the Mediterranean coast to the east. The country as a whole, together with the Balearics (1936 square miles) and the Canary Islands (2894 square miles), adds up to 194,954 square miles, making it the third largest in Europe. Because of the *meseta*, it is second only to Switzerland in its average altitude above sea level (almost 2000 feet).

This rugged highland is bordered by a welcoming coastline which could not offer more. It is as if the seaboard had pressed upward the parched tableland of the interior, handicapped by climate, insufficient irrigation, soil erosion and exhaustion. By contrast, the northern coast is well-tended verdant countryside of thick mists, forests, pastures and lush damp hills, while the Mediterranean coast, aided by irrigation schemes first built by the Romans and augmented by the Arabs, is profligately fertile, growing rice, palms, legumes, citrus fruits, green vegetables, melons, figs, grapes and olives, and now becoming increasingly responsive to the prosperity and tastes of Europeans to the north.

The vividness of this contrast is repeated over and over again as one goes around Spain, looks back through its history or meets Spaniards themselves. There is always the mouth-watering, ripe, civilised and ornate on the one hand, and at no distance the arid, infertile and severe on the other. Such diversity is emphasised by the climate. North of the Cantabrian range, along the narrow strip where Galicia, the Asturias, Cantabria and the Basque country lie, there is a typically Western European climate. Maritime air streams give cloudy skies, frequent rain, mild winters and cool summers, modest daily temperature variations and trees familiar throughout Europe: the chestnut, larch, beech and pine of France, Germany and Austria. There are heavy dews in the mornings, often drizzling rain and poor visibility.

South of the Cantabrian range, making up two thirds of the country, is dry Spain, characterised by scanty rainfall and burning summers relentlessly parching the land for month after month. The jingle "The rain in Spain stays mainly in the plain" is no more true than the Phoenician belief that Spain was an island. Occasionally the sky is darkened by a swift, violent thunderstorm unwanted in Portugal, but the evidence of its passage lasts only briefly and then the sun, from a cloudless sky, resumes its vigil over the desolate expanse of depleted soil. If the rain does last, then it can be counted upon to carry away the topsoil, ravage roads and bridges, and trigger flash floods which will do more harm than good. The Sierra Alhamilla, in the southeastern corner of Spain, is the driest, most desolate and most Saharan of all Spanish landscapes. So much so that many films with desert settings have been shot in the vicinity, including the epic *Lawrence of Arabia*, and numerous spaghetti westerns, not least Clint Eastwood's first step to mega-stardom *A Fistful of Dollars*. At present, and where better, the area houses a solar-energy research project.

Christopher Columbus (Cristóbal Colón).

Different again from the green, densely populated, northern coast and the hot, infertile tableland is the climatically favored Mediterranean coastline which attracts the majority of more than fifty million tourists annually. Understandably, the tourists flock to low-budget bathing resorts and inexpensive wine, creating a growth industry that shows no sign of peaking after thirty years or more. Andalucía and the coast provide the sunlit days and lustrous lights, the tropical vegetation and competitively priced accommodation which helps so much of Europe — and many Spaniards — face long, chilling winters.

Given that only one third of Spain benefits from a reliable and ample rainfall, it is predictable that the rivers with their modest flows contribute very little. There are no huge flood plains or great lakes, so that man-made reservoirs have to eke out the sluggish water-courses. Unlike the many major cities of Europe which owe so much, often their origins, to nearby rivers, Spain has only one inland port, Seville, which is located on the Guadalquivir. It was down river from Seville that Columbus set out in 1492 from Palos de la Frontera, and from Sanlúcar along the coast that the Portuguese navigator Ferdinand Magellan sailed in 1519 to circumnavigate the world. From 1503 until 1680 Seville was granted the legal monopoly for trade with the Americas, distinction enough for a river port, even if incoming gold- and silver-laden galleons gave way, over the centuries, to departing freighters loaded with wood, lead or mineral ores.

Apart from the Guadalquivir, four other major rivers empty into the Atlantic: the Mino, Duero, Tagus and Guadiana, while three others, the

Segura, Lucar and Ebro, drain into the Mediterranean. It is a wry comment on the not untypical river Manzanares, which trickles slothfully past Madrid, that a mayor determined to improve the city in the late 1970s had to inject water into its narrow bed. To see the Manzanares, it is said, you must rush to its banks the moment it rains, otherwise you miss it. If rain is scarce and the rivers unhelpful, the winds are something else. The same southwesterlies which filled the sails of trans-Atlantic adventurers roister still along the western coast, while the Mediterranean shores attract the sirocco, a wind rising in the Sahara that brings both dust and any moisture captured as it crosses the sea.

For all its sunlight, Spain can be forbidding; after all, castles, unless they intimidate the observer, must be regarded as a waste of medieval man's time; similarly, cathedrals have to awe the onlooker so that the divine message is unmistakable. There is a lot about Spain that is forbidding, awe-inspiring and, in the history of the country, deterringly complicated. "Spain not only lost too many foreign wars, it lost its civil wars, and picked the losing Axis side even when it did not go to war," a Spanish friend once summarised. It is as if Spain for long periods entered a monastic retreat, cut off from the rest of civilisation and lost in its own misery. A misery, and to some extent later a penance imposed by General Franco in order to discipline the country. Following his death, the winds of change swept through Spain, now a member of the European Community and, after a hard century or two, eager to make up for lost time.

More than most countries, Spain may be a victim rather than a beneficiary of its geography and history, although, as with all countries, ultimately it is the people who make the best or the worst of what they inherit. The intelligent use of freedom is no easier than the enlightened use of sudden riches — Spain in the sixteenth century in some ways was not unlike Saudi Arabia in the 1970s. Now that dogma and rigidity are giving way to flexibility and buoyancy, Spaniards can look forward to the future with hope and see the past in its proper perspective.

* * * * *

In 1978 Spain promulgated a new Constitution which restored civil liberties and, with great sensitivity and finesse, organised the country into seventeen autonomous communities, fifteen on the mainland plus the Balearic and the Canary Islands. Spain then became a federal state resembling West Germany or the U.S.A., although working within a constitutional monarchy. Each of the seventeen autonomous communities has its own parliament, elected by universal suffrage and given both legislative and executive authority for matters such as finance, education, culture, public works, agriculture and tourism. Official languages in the communities are recognised and their flags may be flown alongside the Spanish flag on public buildings and upon official occasions. Flags, standards, coats of arms, banners and pennants have a particular significance in a country with a proud history, newly won political liberty, and an enduring fascination with the core elements of God, life, death and family. Regional independence in Spain has many badges: language, accent, food, pastimes and songs are all positive cards of identity, and the Constitution of 1978 had finely to blend inherent regionalism with the new national interests.

An indispensable and crucial prelude to reform was the sustained growth achieved by the Spanish economy in the Sixties and Seventies.

1.
This ancient volcanic eruption in the barren Bardenas Reales region of Navarre evokes the swirling skirt of the flamenco dancer.

2.
For good or ill, throughout history the Pyrenees, pictured here at dawn, have effectively separated Iberia from the rest of Europe. The Pico de Aneto (11,168 ft) is the highest peak in an area which increasingly brings Europeans together for excellent skiing. ▶

3.
The National Park of Ordesa, an area of stunning natural beauty in the Central Pyrenees, has been protected by the government since 1918. ▶▶

4.
Islets stud the sea off Pontevedra, on the Galician west coast. This rugged shore has many steep-sided inlets reminiscent of Norwegian fjords. ▶▶▶

Protected from foreign competition by high import tariffs and quotas, the economy boomed while the annual per capita income grew from 362 US dollars in 1960 to a quite staggering $ 4888 in 1979. However, inflation and unemployment were worrying side effects of this prosperity. Agriculture, for example, a traditionally strong sector, had to change following Spain's membership of the European Community. From a total workforce of 3.5 million in 1979, the number fell to under two million in 1985, yet output increased by 67.5 percent. Such figures might well be the cause for self-congratulation among economists, agricultural managers, politicians and government officials, but a 20 percent unemployment level overall is daunting, even if non-agricultural employment in building and business services is expanding and able to sustain recruitment on a regular basis. The most eye-catching phenomenon in the economy is, of course, the tourist industry. In 1987 Spain became the world's largest tourist market, and all the signs are that expansion will continue for some years to come.

Growth has not come without growing pains, one of them being a rise in crime. The *Guardia Civil* has shored-up some extremely inadequate governments and gained an unenviable reputation in the process. Under the new Constitution, autonomous communities can set up their own police forces. So far only the Basques, distinctive in their red berets, have taken advantage of the option, although some municipalities have recruited their own *Policia Municipal*. Perhaps in the past the authority of General Franco was sufficient to keep crime in check and the armed police were an effective visible instrument. Pickpocketing, robbing parked cars and other minor crimes are becoming increasingly common. The big cities are the worst places: Madrid, Barcelona, but also Málaga and Seville. I remember a friend going to a party and being told to take indoors his windshield wipers and hubcaps. He duly took them in, collected them when leaving, and went outside to find his car had been stolen.

Galicia has always had a reputation for providing shores hospitable to smugglers. Now there is growing concern that cigarettes are giving way to the more profitable cocaine. In Guipúzcoa in 1988 1000 kilos were discovered, and a shipment of 36,000 coconuts from Colombia opened in Madrid in 1989 revealed 300 kilos. The Central Narcotics Department suspected that Spain was being used by the Bogota cartel as a warehouse and distribution center for Europe, provoking some Spaniards to wonder whether the law allowing personal possession of up to eight grams of marijuana should be reappraised.

In 1985, the Costa del Sol was threatened by the Basque ETA terrorists, but tourists were undeterred, as the steady increase in their numbers proves. *Euskadi Ta Askatsuna* (ETA) was founded in 1959 in response to the growing curtailment of Basque language, customs and traditions imposed from Madrid by General Franco. From being a bravely rebellious minority bent upon retaining its cultural values in the face of repressive government, the ETA became the voice of political opposition, which swiftly adopted violence as a means of achieving its ends. Several hundred people have been killed, and the land which a century or so ago gave our international vocabulary the word *guerilla*, has also provided a modern urban exemplar. The killing in 1973 of Admiral Luis Carrero, General Franco's most trusted adviser, by a bomb that blew up his car, was a homicidal reminder of the tenacity of this unique minority, without obvious cultural or linguistic relatives, which retains an enduring conviction of

8.
One of the great Roman legacies is the first century A.D. aqueduct in Segovia. Probably built during the reign of Trajan, it has 118 arches of granite blocks laid without mortar or metal cramps for a total length of 818 metres. It still brings water from the mountains. ▶ ▶

5

5.
The cross and the sea, juxtaposed here on the coast of Mallorca, have each played a crucial role in the history of Spain.

6.
The Cathedral of Toledo was built on the site of the Great Mosque. The most splendid of the lovely side doorways is the Puerta de los Leones at the end of the South transept. Guarded by lions and richly decorated with sculpture, it was made between 1458 and 1466.

7.
These cloisters may be seen as a symbol for the embracing arms of the Catholic Church in Spain. For many years there was no political unity in the country. Different kingdoms lived side by side, each with its own laws and administrations, the power of the king was limited and the only truly unifying factor was the Church. ▶

9.
The Royal Palace
(Palacio de
Oriente), Madrid,
built in the mid-
eighteenth century
in late Renaissance
style.

10.
The Royal Palace, Madrid, is no
longer a royal home. The public can
tour its splendid apartments with
magnificent collections of paintings,
works of art, clocks, and a famous
library and armory.

11-16.
The production of decorative glazed titles was a Moorish enhancement of the utilitarian Roman artifact. In Muslim lands the tile achieved its zenith as a decorative medium. Spain firmly established ceramics as an integral element in architectural decoration and transmitted the art to Europe, notably Delft in the Netherlands. Madrid continues the tradition by blending the artistic and the practical on plaques indicating the names of streets.

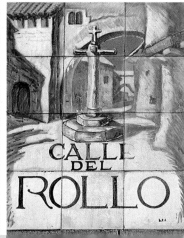

17.
Latin countries brought a grace and playful elegance to the robust English game of soccer. Supporters of Real Madrid, one of Spain's leading teams, often have good reason to celebrate.

18

18.
The Santiago Bernabeu Stadium in Madrid seats 100,000 spectators. The rich Spanish soccer clubs can afford to lure outstanding players from all over Europe and South America.

19.
The exquisite silhouettes of this
poetic skyline are in sharp contrast
with the bustling modern city of
Madrid, only a short walking
distance from the older section of the
city.

20.
On a sunlit evening, Madrileños begin
the ever fascinating exploration of
wine-bars, tascas, and open-air cafés
before their late dinner, at around
10 pm.

21.
The domed church of San Adrés in
Madrid dates from the seventeenth
century. Adjoining it is the chapel of
San Isidoro dedicated to the city's
patron saint, who died in 1170.

22

22.
A wedding in a Madrid church. No
hasty civil ceremony will do for most
Spaniards, who maintain a traditional
Catholic attitude toward the sanctity
of marriage.

23

23.
In the Plaza de la Cibeles, the axis of
the capital, the goddess Cybele,
worshiped as the Mother of the Gods
by the ancient Phrygians, rides in a
chariot drawn by lions, flanked by
spectacular fountains.

24

24.
The Plaza de la Cibeles in Madrid
takes its name from the fountain of
Cybele, a classically-inspired work
from 1780.

25.
After the discovery of America Spain was transformed from a poverty stricken but virile country into a vast but parasitic empire. The Spaniards began building ever grander and more elaborate palaces to display their new found wealth which derived from gold and silver from the New World and the industries of the Low Countries.

26

26.
The Escorial was built by Philip II to fulfill a vow made if he were victorious at the battle of St. Quentin (1557). Comprising a monastery, church, palace, royal mausoleum, library and museum, the enormous complex was completed in 1584 in the presence of the king, who died there fourteen years later.

27

27, 28.
The Escorial library, though modest
in size (c. 40,000 volumes), houses one
of the world's great collections of rare
manuscripts, old maps, codices,
missals and other precious books. Its
magnificent barrel-vaulted ceiling is
decorated with frescoes, mostly
depicting the arts and sciences.

29.
How far these canvases owe their
renown to tales of scandalous
exchanges between the model, the
Duchess of Alba, and the painter,
Goya, is hard to say. Certainly the
'Maja Desnuda' and 'Maja Vestida'
are among the most famous paintings
in the Prado Museum, Madrid's great
national collection of paintings.

30

30.
Spain's greatest painter, Diego
Velazquez, was born in Seville in
1599 and died in Madrid in 1660. In
1634 he painted this magnificent
portrait of the Duke of Olivares, the
ill-fated prime minister of Philip IV.

32.
Sunset behind a statue of Philip II in Madrid. The king abandoned Toledo and the clerics with their persistent interference in state affairs, and in 1561 moved his capital to this city, where he could also better supervise the building of the Escorial. ▶

31

31.
The Royal Palace in Madrid contains a glorious collection of tapestries. There are some 2500 mainly of Flemish production, most of which were collected by Philip V.

its national and territorial rights.

One of the cleverest elements of the 1978 Constitution is the manner in which it supplied the basis for economic improvement while diminishing central direction from Madrid. In the footsteps of the rest of Europe, economics in Spain has outstripped politics in importance; people no longer look over their shoulder in anticipation of the next bureaucratic instruction to their disadvantage. It used to be said: "Everyone works for Madrid, Madrid works for no one," — but no longer. Spain had a lot to do to catch up and achieve her present status of the world's tenth most important industrial nation, the fifth largest in shipbuilding and fourth largest wine producer. From manufacturing motorcars for foreign firms under license, the country gained sufficient confidence and international industrial credibility to produce its own. Principal exports, apart from cars, are petroleum products, iron ore, cork, salt, vegetables, fruits, wines, olive oil, potash, mercury, pyrites, canned fruit and fish, tomatoes, oranges, almonds, peppers and footwear.

The four main cities are the increasingly industrialised capital Madrid (pop. 3,200,000), Barcelona (1,800,000), Valencia (800,000) and Seville (700,000). Together, they account for approximately one sixth of the total population of around 40 million. The industrial revolution hardly touched Spain; now expansion is relentless. Buoyant business investment and construction ensure that the economy is growing at one of the fastest rates in Europe. By July 1989 consumer price inflation had risen to 7.5 percent from a low of four percent the previous year, although the entry of the peseta into the EMS exchange-rate mechanism should have a counter-inflationary influence. It is predictable that strong economic growth will further reduce the rate of unemployment — a major national bogey. The current outlook — the dams, railways, new roads, buildings, watercourses, power plants and factories — spell out change for the old-fashioned and uneconomic sectors of Spanish industry as surely as they do for the Spaniards who, for so long neither corrupted nor stimulated by the world at large, today find American and European materialism increasingly attractive.

THE NORTHERN COAST

GALICIA

Galicia (11,400 square miles) lies in the northwest corner of the Iberian Peninsula. What Spain is to Europe, Galicia is to Spain — a place quite different from the mainland mass. Its four provinces, Lugo, La Coruña, Pontevedra and Orense, clustered together, point toward that final cape, Finesterre ('Land's End'), jutting out in the Atlantic and indicating where prosperity could be found. These are shores of granite cliffs, dropping skeins of mist, cloud-speckled skies, Atlantic westerly winds, and an interior of good agricultural land so free of frost that oranges, lemons and grapes can grow.

The northern coast is sharply nicked with inlets, *rias* or mini-fjords. From these estuaries, which become gentler as they descend southward to Portugal, ply the bulk of Spain's fishing fleet. The catches of cod, sardines and tuna mostly end up in the fish-canning industry centered upon the port of Vigo. Shellfish, crabs and lobsters are also caught around the coast, those not tinned providing delectable dishes on tables in the local restaurants. Land is intensively cultivated: laboriously erected terraces trace the contours of the hillsides. Those heights which prove intractable are abandoned to pines, oak, chestnut and ferns; a quarter of Spain's timber comes from such hilltops.

Galicia is well populated and land scarce. Farmland, although fertile, has been divided and subdivided into ever-decreasing portions, into *munifundias* or fragmented strips too small to be economic or to make the use of machinery profitable. As a result, there is much that is picturesque but agriculturally primitive. Granite walls, essential means of demarcation, take up much arable land and there is obviously scope for change. If Galicia was not already adequately populated, more encouragement might stem from the increasing return of immigrants who sought their fortune in other parts of Spain, in Europe and Spanish America. Their new houses, well located, in good repair and more elaborate than their neighbors', are often indistinguishable from those of the local smugglers who illegally introduce most of the foreign tobacco consumed in Spain. There are growing fears that the smugglers with their high-speed motorboats may find drugs more profitable than cigarettes. Then Galicia, along with the Costa del Sol, would make Spain the main European center for drug distribution — not too far-fetched, given the long-standing Spanish-American connections.

Galicia has its own language, Gallego, owing more to Portuguese than Castilian Spanish. It is one of the most widely spoken of the minority tongues. Vigo, only 25 miles or so from the Portuguese border, is a city with a population of more than a quarter million. Apart from the fishing industry, other commerce includes: ceramics, food processing, glassware, motorcars, plastics, rubber and shipbuilding. The pleasant city of La Coruña is also an important port and oil terminal. In 1588 Philip II dispatched the Invincible Armada from this fine, large harbor to invade England, an enterprise which was harassed by Sir Frances Drake in the Channel, unable to join up with Spanish armies in the Netherlands, and finally destroyed as a fighting fleet by a series of violent gales. Drake sacked the port in 1589 to drive home the victory and divert enthusiasm from a second attempt. Two hundred and twenty years later, Sir John Moore, a forty-eight-year-old British general who had fought in the American Revolution, West Indies, Ireland, Holland and Egypt, Sicily and Sweden, retreated for 250 miles harried by Napoleon's Marshals Soult and Ney and finally defeated them near the seaport before being fatally wounded. Though Sir John Moore was undoubtedly a splendid strategist and leader, his exploits would have been soon forgotten had they not been celebrated by the Irish poet-curate Charles Wolfe in his only poem of note, learned by generations of schoolchildren:

> *"Not a drum was heard, not a funeral note,*
> *As his course to the ramparts we hurried;*
> *Not a soldier discharged his farewell shot*
> *O'er the grave where our hero was buried."*
>
> C. Wolfe, The Burial of Sir John Moore after Corunna

In the province of La Coruña is one of the most historic buildings in Spain, if not Europe, and the world's third holy city, after Rome and

Jerusalem, since an edict of Pope Calixtus II (1119-1124). Santiago de Compostella (Santiago — St. James; Compostella — Field of the Star) acquired its name when a monk was led by a star to the tomb of St. James the Great in 813. Legend has it that St. James, who according to the Bible was beheaded by Herod Agrippa (in A.D. 44), preached in Spain. Despite little historical evidence to support the proposition, Santiago de Compostella became the most celebrated shrine in Europe, attracting as many as half a million pilgrims a year from across the Pyrenees. Chaucer's Wife of Bath sailed to Bordeaux and walked the rest of the way. St. James was venerated in medieval England, and although St. James's Palace is no longer a royal residence, ambassadors are accredited to the Court of St. James. Around the end of the sixteenth century, when the Protestant Drake was at large on the coast, the saint's relics were hidden, lost and forgotten until 1879, when they were found by workmen restoring the church. The sign of St. James was the scallopshell, plentiful on the coast, which was used as a pilgrim's badge in the Middle Ages. Armorial bearings sometimes incorporated the shell, which indicated the standing of those travelers who had journeyed to the Galician end of the known world.

The cathedral's crypt holds the relics of St. James in a silver casket, near the foundations of the original church and beneath the high altar. For some, sight of the casket would have paled by comparison with the outright shock of standing in the enormous rectangular Plaza de Obradoiro and trying to absorb the soaring magnificence of one of the finest cathedrals in Spain. While we may be sceptical about the historical accuracy of the legend, it would be difficult, even in a downpour, to scoff at the buildings. The pilgrimage was a physical and spiritual journey, an opportunity to see the Hand of God and to be enlightened, to learn more of this world and, perhaps, the next. Even if the pilgrim was unmoved by hanging his rags on an iron cross and taking his clothes from the monks, he must have known that the entertainments, the sights, the treasures, the carvings he would see before leaving were an experience unlikely to be repeated in his lifetime.

ASTURIAS

Asturias with an area of just under 4000 square miles is a principality not quite as big as Wales but somewhat similar in terrain, agriculture, industry and the parallel tradition that the heir to the Spanish throne is titled Prince of Asturias, just as the heir to the British throne is titled Prince of Wales.

At the heart of Asturias (often called *the* Asturias) is the triangle of Oviedo, Gijon and Avilés, an important industrial area with the largest steelworks in Spain, lighter metal industries, heavy engineering works, power generating stations and a major bulk-handling port. Mines to the south of Oviedo supply 70 percent of all Spain's pit coal and 15 percent of her anthracite. From the short, turbulent rivers the area generates a surplus of electricity. Agriculture plays its part: the principality is known as the 'dairy of Spain'. There are steep meadows breeding fat cattle interspersed with apple orchards — cider is the local drink on this damp Atlantic seaboard.

With so many other attractive beaches in Spain lapped by warmer waters, the seaside appeal of Asturias is limited, a state of affairs the local population seem content to maintain. It is, however, popular with Spanish holidaymakers. The view that tourism is not the path to prosperity is coupled with a firm determination to preserve the environment, the wildlife and provincial values. The Costa Verde, beautiful and unspoiled though it may be, does not lure the foreign tourists like the Costas Brava, Blanca, del Sol, de la Luz and others, any more than Atlantic cider has the same appeal to foreigners as Mediterranean wine. Some would consider this a blessing.

By 718 Moorish conquest had reached Asturias, where surviving Christian nobles had taken refuge behind the forbidding ramparts of the mountains. Led by the legendary Visigoth Pelayo, the Christians won the battle of Covadonga, checking Moorish penetration into the northwest and setting the stage for eight centuries of strife which ended only with the expulsion of the Moors from Granada in 1492 and the completion of the Reconquest.

Asturians are noted for, and proud of, their stubborn independence and their long history of military resistance to encroachment from Moors, Napoleon or Madrid. It is the kind of courage not unexpected among a people living in a rugged country where mining and quarrying have a history at least as old as Roman times. Perhaps the beautiful mountain chain of the Picos de Europa makes a contribution with its wild gorges, luxuriant green valleys, raw granite edges and snow-tipped peaks. Now climbed for fun, in the past they would have been daunting for dweller and invader alike. Part of the Cantabrian Cordillera, they rise to 8600 feet and offer some of the finest scenery in all Spain. Only an hour or so away by car are long, uncrowded beaches and picturesque fishing ports. Progressive and quietly in control of the lines along which it proposes to develop, Asturias possesses a distinctive blend of coast, mountains, thriving industry and idyllic hamlets which has a changeless appeal.

Philip II.

CANTABRIA

A little more than half a million people live in the smallest, except for La Rioja, of the peninsular communities. Cantabria's chief city is Santander, which used to be the name for the area. In 1941 a fire fanned by a tornado destroyed most of the old town. Today it is a popular holiday resort, particularly for the French, not so much as a center for exploring ancient buildings, of which it has few, as for its unspoiled rocky cliffs, nearby beaches, and general atmosphere of prosperity and cleanliness. The climate is damp, the terrain mountainous and the greatest attraction is probably the Altamira Caves. Because of the need to regulate sightseers, a viewing of the video in the museum is likely to be the closest the visitor gets to their world-famous rock paintings, dating back to the Ice Age some 15,000 years ago. The work of skin-clad nomads, they depict bison, horses, boars and stags with astonishing ingenuity and sureness of line.

East of Santander is the modest fishing-port resort of Santoña, where a monument reminds the visitor of Cantabria's most famous son and one of the may conquistadores little known outside Spain. Juan de la Cosa sailed twice with Columbus, first in 1492 and again in 1498. In a map he drew in 1500 he appears to be the first to question the assumption that the expedition had found Asia. He returned to the Indies in 1501 and again in 1504 to explore the northern coast of South America. He resisted the exploitation of the Indians, which makes his death at their hands, in 1510 on the site of Cartagena, as sad as it is ironic.

THE BASQUE COUNTRY

The Spanish Basque country is the home of two million people. The Basque language is also spoken in Navarre and by 100,000 Frenchmen across the border in Hendaye. There are three provinces, Álava, Guipúzcoa and Vizcaya, which are small, criss-crossed by hills and valleys, fertile, heavily populated, and the most industrialised part of Spain. Bilbao, the capital of the Basques, is the sixth largest city, a major port and center for banking, shipbuilding, engineering, iron and steel, chemicals, cement, and other industries.

The Basques themselves are an enigma. For a start they speak a language that is ancient and unique. Theories abound, although evidence is necessarily scanty, that they may be descendents of Cro-Magnon man. Another theory holds that their forefathers were Central Asian nomads who settled in the Pyrenees out of everyone's way. Euskera — the language — binds this tough, stocky, rather reserved people together; it helped them resist Romans and Visigoths, and maintain a sturdy independence from Spanish hierarchies. In 601, Basques (*Vascones*) occupied Gascony, to which they gave their name, Vasgongadas, but this was a rare sortie out of their homeland; they preferred to be left alone and independent, an attitude prevailing to this day.

The ETA organisation, standing for *Euskadi Ta Askatasuna* (Freedom for the Basque Homeland), is the extremist group of the Basque separatist movement. In recent years it has engaged in terrorist actions, mostly directed against the police, banks and prominent businessman and politicians. Something of the same violence goes into the Basque national sport of *jai alai* or pelota, the fastest ball game in the world, played in a walled court (*frontón*) with a narrow wicker basket attached to a glove, in which the small hard ball (*pelota*) can be hurled at speeds reaching 120 miles an hour.

From the blast furnaces and shipyards of Bilbao it is only 95 miles or so to San Sebastian, the capital of Guipúzcoa, the smallet province in Spain (770 square miles), a town which may have attracted pilgrims on their way to Santiago de Compostella in the Middle Ages but acquired an up-market status as a seaside resort when Queen Regent Maria Cristina stayed there in 1886. A royal summer residence was later built there. The attractions which enticed the Spanish court are the same today: an extraordinarily lovely bay — *Bahia de la Concha* — shaped like an oyster with two hills standing as sentinels and wrapped around by a wide, white, sandy beach. During the Civil War, the fate of the modest town of Guernica, wantonly bombed by the Condor Legion, aroused worldwide revulsion, tinged in Europe by apprehension as to where fascist military might would strike next.

Vitoria is the capital of the province of Álava as well as the seat of the Basque government. As in many old cities, the historic nucleus with narrow streets is perched on a hilltop, while modern suburbs and industry spread out below. Around about are pine-wooded hills, stone houses with low, sloping, slate roofs and, along the Ebro, vineyards producing excellent wine. Although most of the land remains agricultural, there are

Joanna, Queen of Portugal, sister of Philip II.

automotive, steel-making and other industries in the province, concentrated, like the population, on Vitoria.

LA RIOJA

Spain's smallest autonomous community is one of the least densely populated and attracts few tourists compared to some parts of Spain. By contrast, the product for which the area is known travels well all over the world. The wines of La Rioja enjoy an international reputation that has spread with their vigorous marketing and shrewd pricing. Other fruits and vegetables are grown profitably here, notably asparagus, tomatoes and strawberries, but viticulture takes pride of place. The fertile valley of the Ebro is the source of most of the wine, despite the fact that the name of the province comes from the Ria Oja, one of its tributaries. Although the area has a history of wine growing, dating back to pre-Roman times, it was, oddly enough, the plague of phylloxera that gave a fresh boost to its viticulture: when the disease attacked French vineyards, many Bordeaux growers came south and established themselves on the upper reaches of the Ebro.

NAVARRE

Navarre (4022 square miles) is small, has only half a million inhabitants, and is unique among Spanish provinces in retaining its ancient name rather than that of the capital, Pamplona. If the Balkans had not provided a word to describe linguistic, economic, social and historical forces which sustain antagonisms within a region, the Iberian Peninsula might have done so. And if Spain failed the test, Navarre might have succeeded. There is a consistent incompatibility: be it the wet, emerald-green Pyrenean mountains in the northern part contrasted with the drier plains of cereals and vineyards to the south, or in the many people who speak Basque and follow Basque customs, and the fact that the region has been loyal to Castilian Spain and to Madrid (unlike the neighboring Basques, the Navarrese fought on the side of General Franco).

Despite the differences, not helped by a period from 1234 to 1512 when it voluntarily chose a French king, Navarre has the running of the bulls in Pamplona, and what could be more Spanish than that? Pamplona, lodged at the foot of the western Pyrenees, is named after Pompey, the Roman general who was the rival of Caesar and victor over rebels in Spain before returning to Rome to defeat Spartacus. Visitors, Spanish and foreign, flock to the city in July to see the bulls coursed through the streets in the early-morning *encierro*, led by local youths, who play with bravura to the gallery watching from windows, balconies and carefully cordoned pavements. The enraged animals are led from the corral to the bull ring where the corrida is held in the evening. Since the running takes only two minutes or so, it is, of course, only a small part of the feast of San Fermin — the city's patron saint and first bishop, martyred by a bull. For the rest of the time there is good food to be eaten, wine to be drunk, streets to be danced in, and an infectious spirit of good fellowship.

Roncevalles, 30 miles away, is the pass through the Pyrenees, a traditional gateway to and from France, where Roland, the great French hero of medieval legend, was slain in 778. As with most medieval legends, there is some discrepancy between reality and myth. Roland was, in fact, Charlemagne's prefect of the Breton march, who was leading the rearguard of the Frankish army through the pass when they were cut off and destroyed by the Basques, exacting revenge for the sacking of Pamplona. However, the legend makes Roland a nephew of Charlemagne and changes the Basques into Saracens. The *Chanson de Roland* tells of the treason of Ganelon who instigated the Saracen attack, Roland's refusal to blow his horn, Olifant, to summon aid until the death of this friend Olivier, his attempt to break his sword Durandel, his heroic death, the arrival of Charlemagne and the capture and death of Ganelon. It is recorded that the song was sung to the Norman knights as they deployed against King Harold at Hastings in 1066, almost three centuries after the event. The Roland epic caught the fancy of French, Spanish and Italian troubadours; medieval towns all over Europe erected statues to honor the lonely death of a noble warrior trapped in a misty mountain pass by the intrigue of a countryman and the blood-crazed hordes of Islam. Truth may have been a casualty in the retelling of this tale, but the messages were potent and struck a unifying cord throughout Europe in the age of chivalry.

ARAGÓN

The three provinces of Huesca, Teruel and Zaragoza make up this completely landlocked region (18,419 square miles), sided by six other provinces all around and by the Pyrenees and the French border to the north. From the high sunny southern slopes of the Pyrenees the land runs through a sparsely populated central plain, drained by the Ebro. Irrigation, the key to trasforming this former desert, was begun long ago by the Moors but has been greatly expanded in recent years. Zaragoza the capital, the fifth largest city in Spain, is located on the Ebro in the midst of fertile land. Nearby is the familiar tan-coloured terrain of the plateau, sliced by chilling winds in winter and baked by shade temperatures (where shade exists) of 100°F in dehydrating summers. Sheep are raised all over Aragón and cattle in the Pyrenees.

Zaragoza (Saragossa in English) is a corruption of the name of Caesar Augustus, who actively campaigned in northern Spain (25 B.C.). For the eighth-century Moors, the capital became a self-governing caliphate sufficiently strong to drive off the marauding Charlemagne, who sought to extend his sphere of influence and buttress the land south of the Pyrenees against Muslim incursions into France. Later, Aragón was to become an influential kingdom including Catalonia, Mallorca, Sicily, Naples, Athens and Sardinia, although the various possessions were often at war with each other and nothing like as unified as a single kingship would suggest.

Katherine of Aragón, daughter of Ferdinand and Isabella, at the age of sixteen was married in 1501 to Arthur, eldest son of Henry VII of England. Arthur died the next year and she was handed on in marriage to Henry VIII in 1509. Having failed to produce a male heir, she was subsequently replaced by Anne Boleyn but, displaying the stubborn fighting spirit said to be typical of the Aragonese, she defied Henry, kept her head, and died after a long illness in 1536. Not a fruitful dynastic marriage, any more than the marriage of her only daughter, Mary I, to King Philip II of Spain prevented conflict between kingdoms.

33.
The church of St. Thomas (Santo Tomé) in Toledo contains one of El Greco's most famous paintings: 'The Burial of the Count of Orgaz'. This work, completed in 1586, commemorates the nobleman who rebuilt the church and was interred in it in 1323.

Aragonese are supposed to be pretty hardheaded, but they are not without a legend or two to match those of other parts of Spain. It is said that the apostle St. James the Great (who probably never set foot in Spain) passed through Zaragoza on his way to Santiago de Compostella in A.D. 40. St. James converted the townspeople to Christianity and while so engaged, the Virgin Mary descended from Heaven on a pillar and indicated a spot on the bank of the Ebro where he should build a church dedicated to her. The church, one of Zaragoza's two cathedrals and the less distinguished architecturally, has been much reconstructed and enlarged, acquiring in the process blue tiling, and a semblance distinctly Moorish. Inside, on a silver inlaid jasper pillar, is a fifteenth-century, foot-high carving of the Virgin protected by a silver grill. The *Basilica de Nuestra Sénora del Pilar* has given rise to the popular girl's name Pilar. To one side of the Chapel of the Virgin two bombs thrown at the basilica during the Civil War are on display; it is believed they were defused by the Virgin. So legend can be contemporary; appropriate for the province which helped to institute the Spanish pilgrimage enterprise, precursor of tourism, a thousand years ago.

CATALONIA

The northeast corner of Spain has four provinces: Barcelona, Gerona, Lérida and Tarragona. Triangular in shape, it is bordered to the north by the snowy Pyrenees, their slopes clad with thick, green forests, and to the east by the balmy Mediterranean, where the beautiful rocky Costa Brava (Wild Coast) gives way, below Barcelona, to the Costa Dorada, so named because of its long golden beaches. The landscapes, like Catalan customs, language, dances, history and architecture, are far removed from the sobering *sol y sombra* of the Spain of the *meseta*. In the south are the intensely cultivated areas watered by the lower Ebro, producing cereals, olives, vines and a profusion of fruit and vegetables.

Barcelona, the town, is the hub of the most active industrial region in Spain, with a free port zone and industries which provide 22 percent of the nation's output — textiles, paints, chemicals, automobiles, plastics, fertilizers, electrical equipment, machinery and leather. A tide of immigrants from other, poorer, parts of Spain have been attracted to this prosperous region, although with general economic development, Andalusians are giving way to Moroccans and others from Africa, many employed on the construction of roads, buildings and tourist playgrounds.

Probably half the three million inhabitants of the city of Barcelona are not from Catalonia, yet the character of the province is quite distinct. Catalans have always been doggedly determined to retain their own cultural values, their language, their flag (some years ago it was a criminal offence to fly it), and take fierce pride in their history of independence from the rest of Spain, in particular from Madrid. Catalan nationalism has been a constant corrective to rulers who wanted to deploy the region's resources without understanding the deeply felt aspirations of the people.

Barcelona has always been the stronghold for Catalan separatism and was the scene of many insurrections. Later it became the Spanish center of socialism, syndicalism, anarchism and other forms of radicalism, none of which endeared it to General Franco. The city flourished under the Romans and Visigoths, fell briefly to the Moors and was taken by Charlemagne (801), who included it in the Spanish March, a buffer-zone

34.
Standing in a loop of the Tagus, Toledo, ancient capital of Castile, compresses fortifications, palaces, museums and churches into an exciting maze, where swordsmiths still forge their celebrated steel blades. ▶

35.
The historic city of Toledo, a museum in itself, has many fine churches. The building of its great cathedral was begun in 1227. ▶▶

37.
Thanks to the bluff on which much of
Toledo stands, there is no shortage of
vantage points above roof-top level
from which to appreciate the diversity
of architectural styles.

36

36.
The Valle de los Caidos memorial,
some five miles from the Escorial, is
dedicated to the fallen, on both sides,
in the Civil War. Work on it began in
1940 and was completed in 1959.
General Franco is buried there.

38.
As the builders intended, the eyes of the visitor to Toledo are constantly drawn upward to marvel at the ingenuity of design and constructional skill, as here in the cathedral square.

39.
A watermill wheel in Murcia, typical of those introduced by the Arabs, used for power generation and irrigation. Given their desert origins, the Arabs showed great ingenuity in hydraulic innovation.

40.
A bleak slope of the national park in Lérida, the Valley of the Pines. Clad in its winter mantle, it does nothing to suggest the province is renowned for the quality of its fruit and olive oil. ▶

41.
In Cervantes' time, the windmill represented a new industrial technology. Today, here in La Mancha, a windmill is propped up to preserve the landscape immortalised by Don Quixote's exploits.

42.
An exquisitely worked shawl and distinguished hair-style contrast with a blemished wall in the town of Salamanca. Conquered by Hannibal in 220 B.C. and partly demolished in the Peninsular War, Salamanca is a gracious city of the eastern plains.

42

43

43.
La Mancha's windmills now look as
they might have done had Don
Quixote's celebrated tilt resulted in a
victory for the contentious old don. In
fact, the curiosity value of these relics
of Spain's literary past is much prized
and their preservation assured.

47.
Pilgrims' votive offerings at the end of their journey may take many forms. Here on Tenerife, wheat stalks are stylishly arranged as a thanksgiving for the blessings of the soil. ▶

46.
A woman's costume from Ibiza; in the middle of this display of colorful fabrics and ornate jewelry there is a cameo of the Virgin and Child.

44

44.
Like brooms brushing the sky, the palms of Tenerife are one of the many charms of this popular winter destination for Europe's holidaymakers.

45.
Mallorcan windmills differ from the more familiar 'giants' of La Mancha. For one thing, constructors often used a dry-wall technique with trimmed stones aligned with great precision.

45

between France and the Moors. From the ninth and tenth centuries onward, the March became independent under the powerful leadership of the counts of Barcelona, notably Wildred the Hairy, who supported Charles the Bald in the defence of Paris and founded a dynasty which was to rule Catalonia for five hundred years.

Barcelona is agreeably situated on a plain between two mountains and alongside the sea; the summer can be scorching, although enlivened by a breeze off the Mediterranean. The mountains protect the city from the bitter cold winds of the north sufficiently for palm trees to grow. The city is the home of the richest soccer club in the world, possesses a magnificent Gothic cathedral begun in 1298, owns the Picasso Museum containing 2500 paintings, drawings and engravings, and offers to view the controversial Church of the Holy Family (*Templo de la Sagrada Familia*), begun in 1822 and still unfinished.

Never too intent upon making money to find time to appreciate the pleasures of life, Barcelonans are excited by the extensive modernisation program involving a metro line to the Montjuich stadium, site of the Olympic track and field competitions and the opening and closing ceremonies; a new stretch of ring road and the building of hotels. There is a businesslike flamboyance about the preparations to host the 1992 Olympics which are an expression of the bottled-up feelings of the past, as well as a determination to show what Catalans can do. A slogan to be seen and heard everywhere is: "*Barcelona, mes que mai*" or "Barcelona, more than ever", a rallying cry likely to gain a considerable currency as the next decade unfolds.

Tarragona has fertile soil producing superb fruit, vines and vegetables, and a beautifully sited capital, one of Spain's oldest cities, as testified by the remains of cyclopean walls from the third century B.C. It takes no imaginative feat to see why the Romans, who captured it in 218 B.C. and fortified it against the Carthaginians, turned it into a flourishing commercial center and one of the greatest cities of Roman Spain. Having fallen to the Visigoths (fifth century) and the Moors (eighth century), it was recovered for Christian Spain by the count of Barcelona (end of eleventh century), although the splendid cathedral was not begun until a hundred years later. Today, the tankers moored in the bay, the railway, the suburbs, the cranes and the paraphernalia of modern industry impair some of the intrinsic loveliness which caught the fancy of the Carthusian monks who, when expelled from the Grande Chartreuse in 1903, left France to settle in Tarragona and carry on producing their famous liqueur.

VALENCIA

Valencia, the modern autonomous region, is made up of three provinces: Castellón in the north, Valencia, and then Alicante to the south. Four million people live along this narrow 300-mile coastline which averages only 40 miles in width. Inhabited originally by the Ibero-Celts, or Celtiberians, who mined minerals to trade with the Phoenician ships that plied along the coast, the area was later colonised by the Carthaginians and subsequently became a battlefield between the latter and invading Romans. The Moors took over in the eighth century and at the fall of the caliphate of Córdoba (1022), Valencia became an independent emirate. El Cid ruled briefly both the city and the province from 1094 till 1099.

Later, after the conquest of James I of Aragón, the region rose to great commercial and cultural importance, which gradually declined throughout the seventeenth and following centuries.

Clustered around the old city of Valencia is Spain's third-largest urban area, an important center for furniture and ceramics, with newer automobile and steel production expanding rapidly. As a port, Valencia is still relatively modest, but the interior of Valencia and Castellón is agriculturally abundant, producing citrus fruits, onions, rice, potatoes, almonds and vines. The extensive fertile plain — *la huerta* — surrounding the city of Valencia and stretching along the coast was first irrigated by the Romans and then by the Moors, who improved the system. From the paddy-fields of Albufera comes the aromatic rice which is the basis for *paella valenciana*, the region's great contribution to international cuisine.

In the northern part, where the coastline is known as the Costa del Azahar — Orange Blossom Coast — are the orange groves which between November and March produce two million tons of fruit. When blossoming, their fragrant perfume pervades the whole countryside. The Costa Blanca — White Coast — named after the dazzling white light which illuminates the stunning shore, is hotter than anywhere else in Spain, a factor which promotes the area's most lucrative industry by drawing millions of vacationers from all over chilly northern Europe. Benidorm is the undisputed tourist capital of the Costa Blanca, where holidaymakers have precisely the vacation they want at a price they can afford. Two golden beaches, augmented with sand shipped from Morocco, transformed an erstwhile small fishing village into a tourist mecca that cleverly adapts and expands year after year.

Alicante province is a center for the footwear and carpet industries. The port thrives and the airport lands two million passengers a year, many come to enjoy the warmest and most reasonably priced winter holidays in Europe. The palm-lined promenade offers a more traditional aspect of the Costa Blanca than the permanent exuberance of Benidorm, plus a reminder that the visitor is in Spain.

Castellón (pop. 126,000), north of the city of Valencia, is the capital of this province noted for wine, oranges, carob and the manufacture of glazed tiles (*azulejo*). From the tourists' standpoint, it is completely upstaged by the small town of Peñiscola (pop. 3000), built upon a rock only just connected to the mainland by a sandy isthmus. In 1234 James I of Aragón, having captured it from the Moors, gave Peñiscola to the order of the Templars. Their severe, commanding castle has been splendidly restored and in summer twilight looks magical bathed in the blond rays of a setting sun.

MURCIA

Murcia, although the driest region of Spain and quite possibly of Europe, when watered by the river Segura and at its best, is one of the finest garden regions in the country. In the last two or three decades enormous reservoirs have been constructed, irrigating ever greater areas growing apricots, lemons, tomatoes and red peppers. Murcians attract the kind of mocking jokes that the Irish in Britain are familiar with, and like the Irish they have often had to look elsewhere for work or to emigrate. Cartagena, a port and naval base, was the major city of the Carthaginians

EL TORO

in Spain, and they were plainly fond of it, finding the irrigation schemes yielded good crops and the nearby mines, lead, silver, sulphur and iron.

The Segura and its major tributary the Guadaltentin have been tamed by irrigation schemes which distribute water through thousands of miles of channels, and not only aid agriculture but eliminate the threat of widespread flooding. Murcia, the city, lies at the junction of the rivers and provides the commercial and administrative center. Dominated by the tall cathedral tower, it is a charming place full of good restaurants, relishing its autonomy and by no means held in thrall by its antiquities.

THE BALEARICS

Ibiza, Mallorca (Majorca) and Menorca (Minorca), with a total area of just under 2000 square miles, are a group of Mediterranean islands 55 to 125 miles off the Spanish coast. Palma on Mallorca is the capital. As its name suggests, Mallorca is the largest of the islands, with an especially fine climate which drew five million visitors in 1988. Somehow the metamorphosis of the coastline's 100 beaches — Calvia has been named one of the eight most carefully looked-after beaches in the world — and the concentration of hotels along its 125-mile length, has neither harmed the surprisingly rural interior nor spawned ugly structures in response to the pressures of mass tourism. All the islands enjoy a superb climate, clear blue seas, fertile areas for agriculture, plentiful supplies of fish, safe beaches, late-night discos and rather more skillfully-made lines of souvenirs than is usual.

At one time or another most of the adventurous seagoing peoples of the Mediterranean — Phoenicians, Greeks, Carthaginians, Romans, Byzantines and Moors — occupied the islands. The British had their turn on Menorca for virtually the whole of the eighteenth century. In 1936 Mallorca was a Nationalist base for an Italian fleet, while Menorca remained Republican until 1939. Differences not obvious to a tourist are summed up by the locals: "Mallorca looks to Spain, Menorca looks to France, Ibiza looks to Africa".

Valldemosa, on Mallorca, is renowned as the place where Frederic Chopin spent a miserable winter (1838-39) with Georges Sand and her two children when she was thirty-four and he twenty-eight. The tubercular Chopin composed some of his shorter works, preludes, nocturnes and polonaises, while Georges Sand enthused over the captivating setting: "It is one of those views which overpower the spectator because they leave nothing to be desired, nothing to the imagination." Less internationally celebrated is Junípero Serra, a Franciscan missionary born on Mallorca, who went to Mexico in 1749 and then on to California (1769). There he founded numerous missions along the coast that were the genesis of cities such as San Diego, Monterey, San Francisco, Los Angeles and San Antonio. Robert Graves, British poet and novelist (*I, Claudius*) lived at Daya, and D.H. Lawrence stayed at Palma in 1929, from where he wrote vividly, albeit somewhat tartly, to a friend: "The Spanish wine, my God, it is foul, catpiss is champagne compared, this is the sulphurous urination of some aged horse."

Menorca is cooler than Mallorca and the Menorcans rather more relaxed, more likely to join in the tourists' enjoyment of their notably greener island. Dolmen, rough stone structures from megalithic times,

View of the Alhambra, Granada,
engraving by L. Weichardt, late
eighteenth/early nineteenth century.

common in Britain, Brittany and Portugal, are to be found all over the island. The usual invaders followed one another in their invariable order. The British arrived in 1708, attracted by the superb natural harbor of Mahon, which could provide safe anchorage for the fleet when not blockading or capturing ports on the Spanish-French littoral. Admiral John Byng, who was sent to relieve the garrison in 1756, was defeated by the French and returned to face a court-martial. He was convicted of negligence and shot, a sobering reminder of the standards expected of British admirals. The British strongly fortified the entrance to Mahon and named it Georgetown after their king. It was an obvious option for the returning Spaniards, in 1802, to rename it for their monarch, Villacarlos (Charlestown).

Ibiza is the smallest of the Balearics' three major islands and the only one with a river. The rather hilly terrain is studded with groves of pine, almond, olive and fig, infusing a hint of the rustic to go with the maritime idyll of delightful coves, safe sandy beaches, clear sea water, whitewashed houses, cloudless skies and just enough of an ancient Ibiza to entertain the Europeans who flock to the ultra-modern hotels each summer.

ANDALUCÍA

Eight provinces make up Andalucía (English: Andalusia): Huelva is the farthest west, Almería farthest east, with Cadiz, Córdoba, Granada, Jaén, Málaga and Seville in between. The Andalusians number about three million although twice that number lives there, a remarkable population shift since the 1960s, when a million Andalusians left the land which offered so little and promised less; a sobering comment on the second biggest region which for most foreigners, and a good many Spaniards, is where the country begins and ends.

No matter how resistant a traveler may be to the flamboyant, how much on guard against the grand Andalusian legend of the travel agent, it has to be acknowledged that the fabulous is there in abundance. With so much variety there is something for everyone. Fertile alluvial plains are patchworked in pastels with gnarled olive trees, vines, citrus fruits, sugar cane, cereals and cotton; elsewhere barren limestone sierras grudgingly nourish scrub, grass and brambles. Down earthen roads lie villages of dazzling whitewashed houses, built closely to give shade to the narrow streets; above is the Sierra Nevada, backdrop to Granada, with Cerro Mulhacén (11,144 feet), the highest peak in mainland Spain. From one of the popular mountain resorts, it is possible to ski in the morning and bathe on the Costa del Sol in the afternoon. The sounds: castanets, stamping shoes, plangent guitars, cicadas, blithe fountains — even the silences — are as compelling and unique as the smells: orange blossom, sea air from Africa, nut-shell fires, spicy cooking and aromatic wines.

Al-Andalus is the Arabic origin for Andalusia, 'the land of the west', the name given by the Moors who ruled for seven centuries, brought cultivation — apricots, peaches, pomegranates, rice, cotton — and the textile industries; brought their cuisine, architecture, carpets, ceramics, irrigation system, and could not do enough to celebrate their earthly paradise. As much thought went into landscaping the farms as it did into the forms of the gardens and geometry of the spectacular buildings.

Granada was the center of the Moorish civilisation; its Alhambra

('Red Fort'), a citadel palace, embodies fourteenth-century Arab taste, a romantic embroidery of rust-colored brick, perfect proportions, palms and cypresses. (Granada is a corruption of *Karnattah*, which means pomegranate in Arabic and is the symbol of the city). Washington Irving (1783-1859), the American author and diplomat, served in Madrid in 1826 and, apart from a biography of Columbus, wrote *The Conquest of Granada* (1829) and *The Alhambra* (1832), having spent three months in the palace. He is alleged to have encouraged the restoration of this building which, apart from normal wear and tear, had endured Emperor Charles V's inept attempts at renovation and expansion, the demolition of several towers by Napoleon's forces, and an earthquake in 1821.

From the imposing fortifications of the exterior, from square towers, studded doors and immense walls, the visitor retreats inwards to the serenely beautiful courts with splashing fountains and marble colonnades, wanders through chambers sumptuously decorated with painted ceilings, honeycomb domes, richly-colored tiles, and gains an appreciation of the extraordinary refinement of Moorish civilisation. Understandably human, but distressing from the aesthetic standpoint, have been the later Christian embellishments springing from a need to build bigger — the huge adjoining palace of Charles V is the celebrated example. Much architecture was inspired by the need to glorify God in order to erase the Moorish memory. However, when seen by the objective viewer it is the achievements of those retreating artisans, gathered in this last stronghold of Moorish power after the disintegration of the northern provinces, that excite most admiration.

Thousands of miles away and centuries later, Islamic architects conceived and constructed the fabulous Taj Mahal. By comparison, this other exquisite and Indian expression of greatness is serene and impresses by the absence of fortifications. But the Taj Mahal is sterile, the awesome proportions and detail are diminished because no one ever lived there, no human echoes of life haunt the surroundings in the way they do the splendid decadence of the Alhambra.

Córdoba, once capital of Moorish Spain, is dominated by its Great Mosque, one of the most beautiful buildings in the world, designed to divert tenth-century pilgrims from the need to travel to Mecca at the other end of the Mediterranean. For seven and a half centuries the mosque (*La Mezquita*) has been a Christian cathedral, but one glimpse of 850 jasper, granite, onyx and marble pillars with over-arching red and white bands, suggests its origin. Córdoba, famed for its silversmiths and leather craftsmen in the Moorish period, is today an industrial city with a busy center of hurrying people (less hurried in the unrelentingly sunny summer), stylish shop-windows, parking problems and luxury goods. Around the outer suburbs are the spreading factories and high-rise apartments — an obligatory part of any inner-city prosperity.

Seville is a river port in a fertile region — olives, olive oil, cork, fruits, vines and essential oils — with a local industry which includes shipbuilding and aero-engines. The city is to host the World Exposition of 1992, the five-hundredth anniversary of Columbus' voyage and an occasion to celebrate the traditional Seville of gardens, caballeros, fiestas, bullfights, starry serenades and black-lace mantillas. Madrid may be the capital, the traditionally somber head of the country, but Seville has a national responsibility for the heart. A spendthrift's charm goes with it, for Seville had the monopoly of trade with the Americas from 1503 to

1718, before it passed to Cadiz.

The city is undeniably one of the most beautiful in the world, for color, architecture and style have not been lost in the pursuit of the monumental. Of course the monumental is present; the cathedral is the largest Gothic building in existence and the third largest Christian church after St. Peter's in Rome and St. Paul's in London. There are probably more historic buildings in Seville than in any other city in Spain, but the legacy of the past lies lightly on its citizens with their well-developed flair for living. Something must, after all, have inspired four operas: *Don Giovanni*, *Barber of Seville*, *Marriage of Figaro* and *Carmen* (the massive Royal Tobacco Factory where Carmen was employed is now part of the University of Seville). And nothing is lost if the style of the operas (*Carmen* excepted) is *buffa* rather than *seria*, any more than the quality is diminished because the composers were neither Spanish nor visited Seville.

The cathedral was begun in 1402, a considerable act of faith, as was the origin of most medieval cathedrals, for those who saw the beginning were unlikely to be present at the completion. Seville cathedral is no exception, partly because of the sheer size and partly because of the lavish standards set by the clergy, who throughout intended to create — and did — one of the great splendors of the country. King Ferdinand III — the Saint (canonised four centuries after he died), liberator of Seville from the Moors, is buried there with his queen. So is Christopher Columbus, his glorious mausoleum set beneath the arching vaults, bestowing dignity on his final resting place. For Columbus, who achieved so much in his lifetime and faced disgrace as well as triumph, not least being shipped home from Haiti in chains, died neglected in Valladolid, bitterly dejected by his treatment and the manner in which his courage, perseverance and navigational skill had been forgotten. His body was taken from Valladolid to Santo Domingo, then to Haiti. When, at the beginning of this century, Spain lost the very last of her American conquests, Columbus' remains were brought back to the city that profited most from his greatness.

All too credibly the cathedral was built on the site of a mosque, but creditably a colossal tower, the former minaret, was retained. This is the famous Giralda, erected upon Roman foundations in the late twelfth century. In 1578 a five-story bell tower was added, surmounted by a statue of Faith, eleven feet high and weighing one and a quarter tons. This statue rotates in the breeze and explains the name Giralda (*girar* — to rotate).

Near the cathedral is the Alcázar, the Mudéjar palace built in the fourteenth century by Pedro the Cruel (second only to Vlad the Impaler, in my mind, as a soubriquet calculated to excite intense curiosity or a desire to pass quickly on). The Alcázar has been lived in; Ferdinand and Isabella received Columbus there, the Holy Roman Emperor Charles V dwelled there, in 1830 Isabella II (who attracted no repeatable soubriquet, but before exile to France in 1870 never allowed affairs of state to deflect her nymphomania) was born there and subsequently returned. A good deal of restoration has been, mostly tastefully, completed on the main buildings, and in anything approaching warm weather, the welcoming gardens are a tranquil haven of greenery and ornamental fountains.

Andalucía has everything in abundance — the subtropical crops in the valley of the Guadalquivir; the wheat in the plains; copper, manganese, iron and sulphur in Huelva; the Costa del Sol; and enough history for

Thousands of pilgrims from all over western Andalucía gather every year on foot, horseback and ox-carts for the feast of Our Lady of the Dew. Masses are celebrated, but the evenings are given over to flamenco and the delights of the fiesta.

49.
Whitsun in Huelva is a time of pilgrimages to local shrines, some of them made in ox-drawn carts like these. Competition is keen to make every wagon as colorful and distinctive as possible. ▶

50.
With the fiesta, Spain has invented an unbeatable formula for public merrymaking. Andalusians are particularly good at organising fiestas that retain a religious flavor while providing fun for everyone. ▶ ▶

51.
The Virgin Mary is greatly venerated in Spain, and nowhere more than in Huelva, where her shrine is carried through the streets accompanied by thousands of pilgrims. ▶ ▶ ▶

52.
Even the essential solemnity of pilgrimage cannot curb for long the spontaneous gaiety characteristic of almost every Andalusian gathering. ▶ ▶ ▶ ▶

53.
It is not hard to imagine all the hours, money and eternal discussions involved in devising and making fiesta finery. The chance of meeting someone in an identical outfit is extremely remote. ▶ ▶ ▶ ▶ ▶

an area ten times the size. Yet, with so many blessings, uneven handed share of prosperity and unchangingly traditional father-to-son methods of farming forced generations of Andalusian peasants to seek work elsewhere in Spain or abroad. Even today Andalucía has the highest unemployment figures for the whole of Europe. But that is a statistic that can change, unlike the spectacular scenery, spellbinding buildings and unique cultural heritage.

THE CANARIES

The archipelago of the Canaries (Islas Canarias) falls into two groups: to the west, Tenerife, Grand Canary, La Palma, Gomera and Hierro; to the east, Lanzarote, Fuerteventura and six islets. Together they make up two provinces, Las Palmas and Santa Cruz de Tenerife, with 1.3 million inhabitants. Las Palmas of Gran Canaria is the biggest city, having almost half the island's total population (750,000). In addition, its port of La Luz, outside the town, is the busiest in Spain and one of the busiest in the world, handling some 50 million tons of shipping each year. Tenerife, however, is the largest island (795 square miles) and has Spain's highest mountain, the Pico de Teide (12,172 feet), snow-clad above 8000 feet from November to April.

Canaries do come from the Canary Islands, although Pliny mentions that the isles were so named because of the number of dogs (*canes*) to be found there. Most of the year a northeast trade wind keeps the climate warm and dry with sunshine enough to attract three million tourists a year and a considerable colony of foreign residents. Volcanic in origin, the islands are too arid, rocky or steep to provide much land for agriculture, though extensive terracing was carried out in the nineteenth century. The rich soil, where it exists, can sustain crops ranging from bananas, oranges, coffee and tobacco, to wheat, potatoes, tomatoes and grapes. Further up the hillsides there are figs, walnuts and almonds. Fishing is an important local industry. On Gran Canaria the mountainous northern interior is noticeably cooler than the noisy, congested city of Las Palmas, especially at night. The south of the island has very little humidity and is climatically almost a semi-desert.

The Arabs knew about the Canaries and established trading posts around A.D. 1000. Later, Genoese, Portuguese and French navigators made landfalls; Spanish sovereignty was only established in the 1490s. Columbus stopped in the Canaries on his first trans-Atlantic voyage. Subsequently the islands became an important staging post for Spanish trans-Atlantic trade, attracting and defeating both Sir Francis Drake and Lord Nelson. Drake was driven off from an assault on Las Palmas harbor while Nelson, in pursuit of a Spanish treasure ship, assaulted Santa Cruz on Tenerife in August 1797 with four ships-of-the-line and three frigates. The first attack was unsuccessful so Nelson decided to lead in person a second foray at night. As his open boat was about to land, the Spanish opened fire; Nelson had his right arm shattered and later amputated. In an amazingly courteous conclusion to the affair, there was a parley; British troops ashore were allowed to withdraw, there was an exchange of Canarian wine and bread for English beer and cheese, and the British squadron withdrew, its commander convinced that a one-armed admiral would be of no further use to the Royal Navy. His

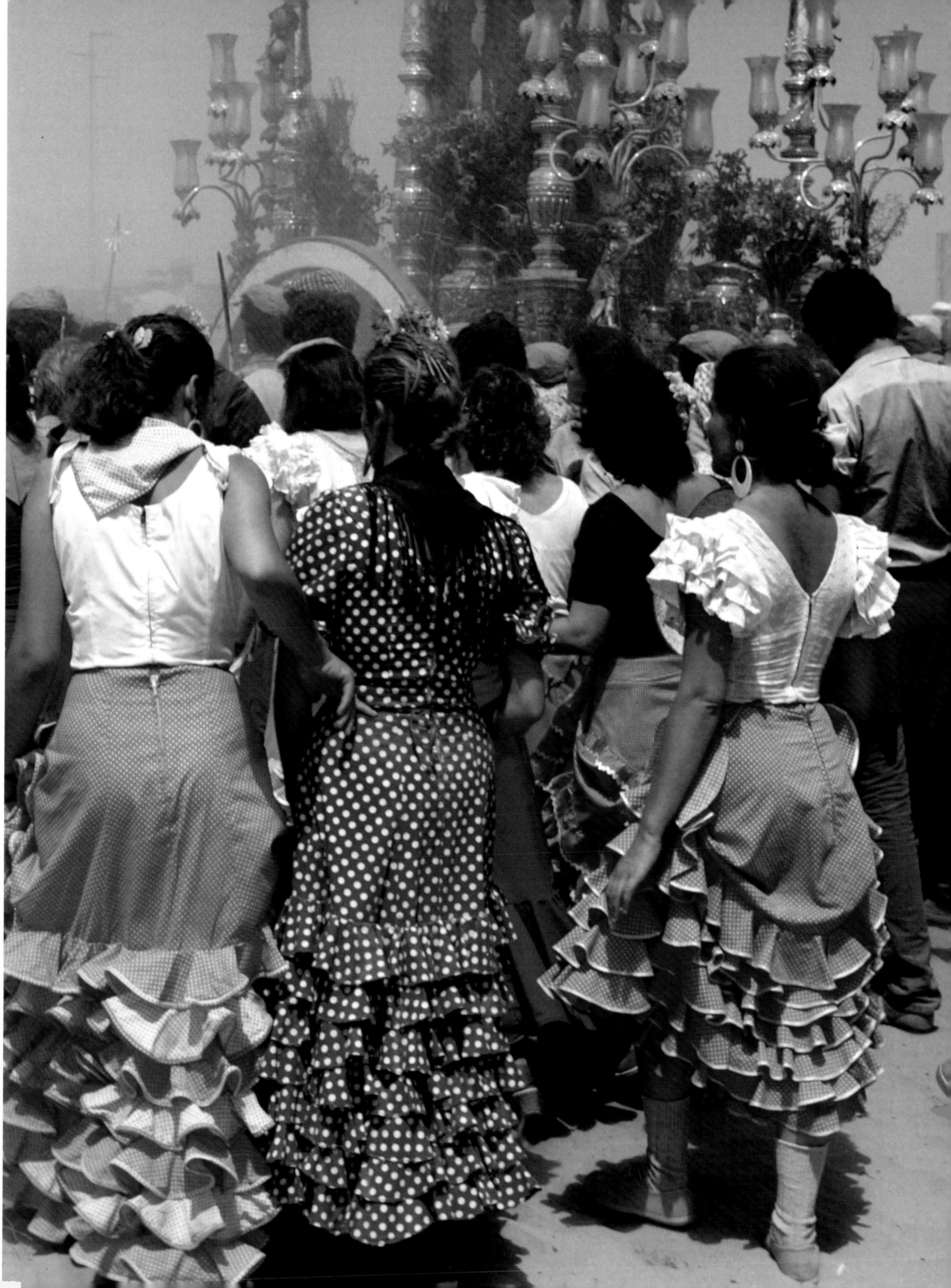

54

54.
The progress of this shrine of the
Virgin Mary at a feast in Huelva
carries echoes of a much older, pagan
ritual, in which the earth goddess was
drawn on a bullock-cart.

55

55.
The image of Christ carrying the cross
is borne through the streets of Gerona,
famed for its cathedral, one of the
finest buildings in Catalonia.
Napoleon conducted a six-month
siege of the city when he invaded
Spain in 1809.

56.
The hill-top chapel of Santa Cristina de Lena (905-912), richly decorated in the Visigothic style, is one of many ancient small churches in the province of Asturias.

57

57.
No disrespect was intended when the
bearers of this statue of the crucified
Christ decided to take a rest in the
welcome cool of wayside greenery
during a lengthy procession at Ujué
(Navarre).

58.
A priest walks in the cloisters in Guadalajara, the modest town (pop. 57,000) which gave its name to the Mexican city so often celebrated in song.

59.
These Romanesque horseshoe arches in the crypt of the little church of Santa Cristina de Lena illustrate the skill of Asturian stonemasons and their determination that their faith would endure in this western outpost of Christianity.

60

60.
San Migual de Lillo in the mountains of Asturias is another of the remarkable little early medieval churches in the principality.

61.
'Caparisoned in splendor and girded with praise', the words of the old hymn, take on a special meaning in Huelva, where the local citizens celebrate the Salida de la Vergen with a penitent sobriety rather than the usual flamboyance. ▶

pessimism proved unfounded.

The great attraction to the tourist is the 'Eternal Springtime' of the climate, with a temperature fluctuating between 64° and 81°F. As in the Caribbean, wintering in the Canaries is definitely more chic than a summer vacation there. The islands offer excellent hotels and bathing, sports amenities and unspoiled scenery, beside several lively resorts.

Until 1927, the archipelago formed a single Spanish metropolitan province. It was then divided because of the rivalry between the ports of Las Palmas de Gran Canaria and Santa Cruz de Tenerife, which then became the two provincial capitals. This division was maintained in the Constitution of 1978.

CEUTA AND MELILLA

There are two remaining enclaves on the Moroccan coast which are a part of Spain. Both are military bases. Ceuta is a duty-free zone and has large ship-repairing facilities. Melilla is further away, less frequently visited, and rather more often mentioned in the press as a town where Arabic-speaking members of the population persistently seek expanded facilities for the teaching of their language in schools and acknowledgement of their religious observances as a constitutional right. There is a mainly Spanish population in Ceuta, which is why the town is not part of Morocco — an issue not devoid of similarity with the controversial question of Gibraltar.

CASTILE AND LEÓN

Until the early 1980s 'Old Castile' (Castilla la Vieja) was the ancient kingdom, the great windy anvil that forged resistance to the Moors as well as the Reconquest which followed. The many castles gave its name to this territory, home of an austere, proud, lean-faced people who, in turn, gave tradition, faith, language and a culture to the nation. On February 25, 1983, Old Castile became Castile and León, the largest (36,000 square miles) and one of the most thinly populated of the new autonomous communities. Santander, an outlet to the sea, was lost to Cantabria and in its place came León, another dry, wind-swept plateau region, crossed by the Duero and its tributaries. Along with cereal-growing plains are sheep; many of the richer mineral deposits have been exhausted. Historically, León can claim to have been in the forefront of the drive south to expel the Moors although success saw the eclipse of León and the gradual rise of Castile as the dominant partner. Nine provinces: Ávila, Burgos, León, Palencia, Salamanca, Segovia, Soria, Valladolid and Zamora, together make up this new heir to an ancient patronage.

Ávila is the highest (3700 feet) and one of the smallest provincial capitals. Its famous walls, constructed by order of Alphonso VI in 1090, stand perfectly preserved, over a mile and a half long, with 88 round towers along the rectangular sides — a brooding, chilly encampment from which most military threats have been removed for nine centuries. Not a cheery place, yet one that powerfully evokes the Middle Ages in a small city on the Castilian plain. St. Theresa (Santa Teresa) was born in Ávila and joined the Carmelite order in 1536. Although a visionary, contemplative mystic and writer, she was also a vigorous reformer, after a vision of the Virgin instructed her to return the Carmelite order to its regime of poverty and simplicity. Wearing sandals instead of shoes became a symbol of the reformed order, the Descalzolos or Barefoot Carmelites. One of the most remarkable women of all time, St. Theresa was the founder of innumerable monasteries and convents, inspired by that other great mystic, Saint John of the Cross. Astute, courageous, occasionally blunt, she was a tireless manager and a writer who could be brisk and wise in her letters or rhapsodic in her meditative treatises. On occasion she could also be uncompromising, as when she asked for divine assistance at a flooded riverside. "That is how I honor my friends", her Inner Voice intimated; "Which is why you have so few", she pointedly replied.

Burgos, the first capital of the kingdom of Castile and now the capital of the province, is far nore lavish than Ávila. It is the birth and final burial place of El Cid, whose remains and those of his wife, Ximena, were re-interred beneath a simple slab within the cathedral in 1921. The great Gothic cathedral, mostly thirteenth-century, is one of Spain's finest, an awesome, soft grey stone edifice, full of religious treasure and sober veneration. Irrigated by the headwater of the Ebro, the province supports substantial agriculture while the town itself has absorbed a commericial sector into expanding suburbs. Like most of the cities of Old Castile, its population has been growing through migration from the countryside.

León is the biggest and most densely populated of the provinces. Its capital, also named León, is a gracious walled city with a hint of French elegance in the horse-chestnut trees screening the boulevards. The same joyous elegance distinguishes the cathedral, considered by many the loveliest in Spain. Originally a Roman camp providing quarters for the Seventh Legion which guarded the plains and a gateway to the north, in the Middle Ages León was an important trade and crafts center on the pilgrim route to Compostella and a seat of the kings of León and Castile. The cathedral was begun in 1205 and completed in the fifteenth century. As with so many artifacts of great beauty, there was an accompanying fragility, which necessitated a major strengthening program in the nineteenth century. One cause of the fragility was the vast stained-glass windows, filling 6500 square feet and allowing multicolored shafts of light, symbolising divine radiance, to filter down upon the fine wood-carvings and precious metals.

Salamanca province is in the south of the region, toward the western edge of the *meseta*. Landscapes are big, fighting bulls are raised locally, and the capital, Salamanca, is an utterly beautiful city of mellow sandstone, probably the loveliest of the famous sister cities of the plateau. Beside it flows the river Tormes spanned by a Roman bridge with twenty-six arches, a reminder that the city's history goes back to the time when Hannibal conquered Salamanca in 220 B.C. The University, for which the city was famous from the thirteenth century onward, bore comparison with Oxford, Paris and Bologna. Columbus consulted the faculty of astronomy before his departure. Partly demolished by the French assault in 1811, the city was liberated by the Duke of Wellington the following year. The admired scholarship — Salamanca University made Arabic philosophy available to the western world — has perhaps diminished, but the presence of thousands of students makes for a lively environment. Among the many outstanding buildings are the two cathedrals, standing side by side. The older, the *Catedral Vieja*, begun in 1160 by Don Jerónimo de Perigeaux and finished a century later, is an outstanding example of the Romanesque style. Don Jerónimo had been chaplain to El Cid, which may account for walls being ten feet thick. The larger *Catedral Nueva*, mostly sixteenth-century, is an impressive late-Gothic structure. Adjoining it is the main square, *Plaza Mayor*, one of the largest in Spain, which used to double as a bullring.

Valladolid, as a province, is a flat, monotonous endless plain of cereals studded with innumerable castles, as one would expect in the very heartland of Castile. The name of the city comes from an Arabic phrase meaning 'town of the governor', and it was the seat of many rulers of Castile before Madrid was established as the national capital. Valladolid has seen historic figures in plenty: it was here that Columbus died in 1506, King Ferdinand married Queen Isabella in 1469, Philip II set out in 1554 to marry Mary Tudor, Queen of England, Charled V reigned and abdicated in 1556, Cervantes wrote the first part of *Don Quixote*. Napoleon's brother Joseph, when king of Spain, was installed in Valladolid until Wellington drove him out in 1813. The splendor of the other cities is missing; somehow the historic past is less vibrant. Though Philip II was born in Valladolid, it was he who started the decline in the city's fortunes by his decision in 1561 to take the capital to Madrid.

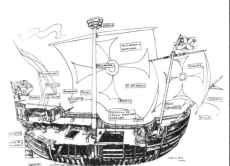

MADRID

The small province of Madrid (8000 square miles) is *meseta* surrounding the capital of almost five million people. It may be its altitude (2000 feet, the highest capital in Europe), coupled with a Mediterranean brightness in the skies and tolerable climate that give *Madrileños* their celebrated vivacity and humour. Madrid was made the permanent capital by Philip II in 1561. He may have thought it easier to start afresh rather than choose one of the rival Castilian candidates, all eager to be first among equals; in 1521 those same cities had revolted against government encroachment on their liberites and could prove sensitive about such issues. The Madrid option has been copied: Bonn, Washington, Canberra, Brasília and Abuja, for example. It certainly worked out for Spain, where the capital at the very center of the Iberian Peninsula serves as the hub of state administration, banking, communications, and an agreeable location for the headquarters of many Spanish and international companies. Enormous sums have been spent to brighten up an intrinsically green, attractive and spacious city which had become one of the most polluted in the world. The Prado Museum is among the world's finest art galleries, the bullring the biggest in Spain, the churches seem without number, and the topics for museums infinite.

The Escorial, or San Lorenzo el Real del Escorial, some thirty miles northwest of the city, originally conceived as a combined monastery, palace and royal mausoleum, is now a world-famous museum with a magnificent library. On a scale befitting the sixteenth-century Spanish empire (eight acres, 16 courtyards, 300 rooms), was built (1568-84) to the orders of Philip II with a remarkable austerity, tranquility and lightness — 2700 windows may contribute. For fourteen years this God-fearing monarch ruled from his modest apartment here over the richest and most powerful nation of that age.

Perhaps the last word, or most recent, in monumental building is the

Valle de Los Caidos (Valley of the Fallen), a memorial to the victims of the Civil War. A tunnel into rock leads to a great underground basilica, 820 feet long. Above it soars a massive stone cross 492 feet high and weighing 200 tons. General Franco, who chose this site near the Escorial, is buried there beneath a plain stone slab. A Benedictine monastery and school are part of the monument, bringing together a leader, war, monumental architecture, and the Church in a tradition as old as Castile.

In 1988 the Union Bank of Switzerland ranked Madrid as more expensive than Paris, an indication of the many changes taking place. *Madrileños* are dismayed at the cost of living and in a recent survey, when asked to name the three topics of most concern, placed it above the increasing crime rate and traffic congestion. It is a noisy capital; an OECD survey made it the noisiest in Europe. Two factors are the police and ambulance sirens, which at moments seem likely to cause brain damage among those within earshot. Since most Spaniards conduct a normal conversation like the preliminaries to mortal combat, or so it sounds to foreigners, they may not find the noise level equally disturbing.

Problems aside, modern Madrid has a vivacity, a relish for newly experienced freedom and an abiding belief in artistic values: soon the Thyssen Art collection will find a home in Madrid: the *Teatro Real* is to become an opera house again; the National Auditorium has been opened for orchestral performances; the National Theater Company and two state ballets have homes of their own; and by no means least, approval has been given for film studios at Pozuelo, twice the size of Rome's famous Cinecittà. All this, in addition to an enormous program of reconstruction, is designed to show Madrid at its finest when in 1992 the city will be the cultural capital of Europe.

CASTILE AND LA MANCHA

Castile and La Mancha (over 30,000 square miles), the third largest autonomous region, comprises five provinces: Albacete, Ciudad Real, Cuenca, Guadalajara and Toledo. Traditionally known as New Castile (Castilla La Nueva), the area provided kings, warriors, a dialect and a literary language. The grandeur of its past is witnessed by the beauty of its cities, mostly set in unprepossessingly bare landscapes.

In the north are the verdant Guadarrama Mountains, which soon give way to the vast *meseta* tableland, watered by rivers such as the Tagus and Guadiana. Stretching to the south is La Mancha, where irrigated cornfields refute its name (taken from the Arabic *manxa* meaning parched), as do the lavish vineyards of Valdepeñas. In the late sixteenth century windmills, a high technology developed in Holland, were built to grind corn grown locally. Don Quixote, who stood for conservative values, tilted at these unfamiliar imports from the outer reaches of the Spanish empire. To the east are the rocky peaks and precipitous gorges of Cuenca, which is sparsely inhabited, like the whole region, the not-unexpected result of scorching summers and biting, wind-driven snow in winter, for there are more welcoming and hospitable parts of Spain not too far distant.

For centuries Moors and Christians fought bitterly across Castile, a name derived from the numerous castles — *castillos* — mostly built by Christian nobles from the eighth to ninth centuries onward. Guadalajara is a province liberally dotted with the often surprisingly substantial remains of fortifications, expressing in stone something of the turbulence of those times, when the expulsion of the Moors vied in importance with the dynastic conflict between Castile and Aragón. Ciudad Real ('royal city') has so little to show it is difficult to see why the battles were so bitter or protracted. This was a buffer zone, a no-man's land in which in 1158 the order of Knights of Calatrava was founded by Cistercian soldier-monks to fight the Moors. Though the order was abolished in the sixteenth century the title of Grand Master is still held by the Spanish sovereign.

Forty or so miles southeast of Madrid is Toledo, a city with a reputation and legends enough for all of Spain, let alone Castile. In a desert tinged with green, half embraced by a comforting bend in the Tagus, the city is today a segment and a memoir of the Church Militant in the Middle Ages. For the better part of four centuries (712-1085) the city was under Muslim rule. In 1085 it was one of the first to be retaken, and when King Alphonso VI of Castile triumphantly entered, at his side rode the legendary mercenary Rodrigo Díaz de Vivar, nicknamed *El Cid Campeador* 'the Conqueror'. Whether he was as chivalrous as the 3700 verses of *The Song of El Cid* suggests, or had the stature of Charlton Heston, we shall never know, but the image of the embodiment of national virtue, of all that was finest in Spanish or Castilian virility, took on an epic life of its own, combining the gifts of a brilliant soldier with those of a shrewd politician caught up in fluctuating alliances along a religious frontier. As potent as the legend of El Cid is the tradition of the Toledo steel blade (manufactured by a technique brought from Damascus), evoking the skill and artistry of the sword-makers as well as the bloodiness of the use to which it was put. The vestige of this craft is seen today in the arrays of inlaid-steel wares offered to tourists as expensive souvenirs of a day-trip from Madrid.

ESTREMADURA

Estremadura, its name thought to be derived from the Latin *terra extrema et dura* ('an extremely hard land'), although it could mean 'beyond the Duero River', lies to the west of Spain and borders Portugal. Its two provinces, Badajoz and Cáceres, are sparsely populated and unusual in lacking any access to the sea. To the north are the lovely Sierra de Gredos and to the south the gentle chain of the Sierra Morena. A part of the *meseta*, when watered by rivers such as the Alagón, Guadiana, Tietar and Tagus, the region can be surprisingly fertile, providing cotton, wheat, tobacco, fruit and vegetables. Up into the hills go the great flocks of sheep when the plains bake under a relentless summer sun. Storks' nests precariously ornament every high place, and below are whitewashed villages which draw together the scattered inhabitants. A vigorous attempt to inject life into the area began in 1952 with the inauguration of the 'Badajoz Plan' and the settlement of 8000 families on small holdings of ten to twelve acres along the Guadiana River, coupled with the building of irrigation dams and large reservoirs.

Perhaps economic necessity impelled conquistadores such as Cortés and Pizarro to leave this arid tableland, although the absence of a seaboard was unlikely preparation. They may have been natural soldiers, for generations had fought against the Moors. A compulsion to profess

Christianity to non-Europeans half-the-world away may have been a factor. Whatever the cause, they displayed great courage setting off in small bands upon frail ships, as well as ruthless brutality to one another and toward those they conquered. Small bands they were, and in the case of the Pizarros, a band of brothers, but the ties of kith and kin were often as little regarded in the expanse of the New World as they were in the shifting loyalties of the homeland. Francisco Pizarro, conqueror of Peru, was an illiterate pig-keeper and bastard son of a gentleman of Trujillo. His legitimate half-brother, Hernándo, was unique among the five brothers since he died in bed, one chronicler says at the age of a hundred.

Other *Estremeños* left their mark on the New World. Hernán Cortés, born in the small town of Medellin, conquered Mexico in spite of the Spanish administration in Cuba and lukewarm encouragement from Charles V. Hernándo de Soto landed on the Florida coast in 1539. Together with his small band he moved north to Georgia and the Carolinas into Tennessee, turned south into Alabama, and after re-equipping set off again in 1541, crossing the Mississippi, journeying up the Arkansas River into Oklahoma, then back to the Mississippi, where he died. He was forty-two. Vasco Nuñez de Balboa, after a heroic march across the Panama isthmus and conciliation with Indians, declared that all the shores washed by the waters of the Pacific Ocean, which he had discovered, were claimed for the Spanish crown. While preparing an expedition for Peru in 1519, he was seized, accused of treason and beheaded. He was forty-four. Pedro de Valdivia, one of Pizarro's best officers, educated, energetic and less cruel or avaricious than most of his colleagues, conquered Chile. In 1553 he took forty men to stamp out a rebellion and was wiped out by the rebels. He was fifty-four. After serving as lieutenant to Gonzalo Pizarro, Francisco de Orellana, another native of Trujillo, was the first to explore the Amazon. He died on a further expedition up the great river, which took its name fron Orellana's account of a skirmish with female warriors (long-haired Indians mistaken for Amazons). He was forty.

The *nouveau riche* conquistador, just back from the New World with his winnings, may have extravagantly embellished his mansion and adorned it with huge coats of arms, but he was in a very perilous line of business. If, on his next voyage, he did not fall foul of the understandably upset American Indians, there was every chance either his loot or his life could be forfeited as a result of intriguers at court or in the colonies. Cáceres is a town where the *hidalgos* or gentlemen-soldiers came home to flaunt their wealth and exchange their sagas. Trujillo was another such town, and emphasises the point with a magnificent equestrian statue of Francisco Pizarro dominating the main square. Badajoz, on the other hand, shows more signs of the invaders from Rome and North Africa and, in the modern apartment blocks, something from Madrid. Mérida was founded in 23 B.C. as a frontier town, Augusta Emerita, for a Roman legion. A surprising amount of their construction evaded later Moorish builders, including a theater seating 4000 built by Marcus Agrippa, a Roman circus which will hold 30,000, an arch celebrating Trajan, and a temple of Diana. It also has a central street named after John Lennon, who once considered he was better known than Jesus Christ.

Guadalupe has one of the most famous monasteries in Spain, founded by Alphonso XI of Castile on a site where a cowherd discovered a statue of the Virgin said to have been carved by St. Luke. The tiny town (pop. 2800) lies in an alpine setting, dominated by the fourteenth-century monastery which gave its name to New World pilgrimage churches (notably in Mexico City) and to an island discovered by Columbus which became part of the French Caribbean. Upon returning home, pious conquistadores enriched the church, which was used for the baptism of the Indians they brought with them. A great deal was taken from the New World; it is a paradox that so much that has endured in Latin America should have come from the veneration of an Estremaduran wooden image of the Virgin. More understandable, perhaps, is the presence in the monastery of a profusion of jeweled robes, miniatures, illuminated manuscripts, chalices, gold-embroidered vestments and paintings, all visible signs of the medieval barter of the spiritual for the material.

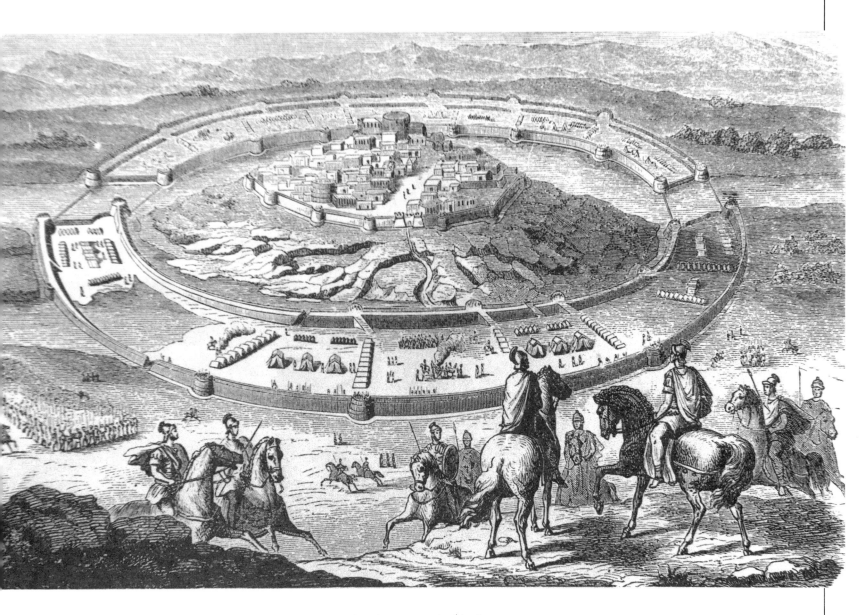

The Celtiberian stronghold of Numantia (near modern Soria) which fell to the Romans in 133 B.C., engraving.

Land of History

Before the Moors: the oldest Spain

Neanderthal man left behind his weapons and charred animal bones in Spain, notable near Soria (Madrid), which suggests that he might have moved across the Pyrenees during advances and recessions of the polar ice-cap. Prehistoric man left his mark in the caves at Altamira and illustrated a first chapter in the history of the land. Other cave paintings at important sites near Valencia show not only animals but early man himself, hunting, herding and fighting. The men wield bows and arrows while the women are distinguished by wearing only long bell-shaped skirts.

Around about 2500 B.C. the neolithic society gave way swiftly as men in the south began to work in metals — first copper, then bronze — and developed a variety of skills relating to agriculture, animal husbandry and mining, trading with other Mediterranean peoples, not least with the Aegeans. Fortified hilltops distinguish the culture which spread northward, impressively raising wheat, barley, grapes and olives; using domestic animals such as dogs, sheep, pigs and horses. The same people built distinctive burial chambers. One in particular, at Anteguera (an hour or so from Málaga) has 31 stone slabs with a combined weight of 1600 tons. This dolmen culture with its easily recognisable megalithic monuments spread throughout Western Europe, reaching Portugal, Italy and Sardinia, as well as North Africa. Some authorities consider dolmen were erected for use as tombs.

Iberians, who may have migrated from North Africa, introduced a strong economy based on agriculture, mining, animal husbandry and fishing, and produced textiles, jewelry and pottery. This led to increased trading in the Mediterranean and a population growth, accompanied by the appearance of larger settlements, some worthy of the name of towns. Cremation was widely practiced and excavated burial grounds have revealed a rich variety of weapons, pottery and grave furnishings.

Phoenicians, the great seafaring traders, began to take an interest in Spain around 1000 B.C. It may have been a Phoenician vessel in which Jonah, the eighth-century B.C. prophet, was sailing to escape the wrath of God when he was swallowed by a whale (Jonah 1,3). Jonah sailed for Tarshish, then a rich Spanish city on the Atlantic coast which has never been satisfactorily identified. According to the Book of Kings, "Jehosaphat made ships of Tarshish to go to Ophir for gold"; Solomon also sent ships to Ophir to bring tribute of fine gold, precious stones, ivory, apes and peacocks. The location of Ophir, possibly India, Sri Lanka or Arabia, is unknown, but it would seem that long-distance voyaging of mariners from Spain had very early origins, and familiarity with the bulk shipment of prized cargoes began long before the galleons anchored off the Panamanian isthmus. Tarshish of the Bible, the Tartessos of Greek and Latin

62.
Moors and Jews were both expelled from Spain. In Córdoba the Moors left behind their Great Mosque, one of the finest achievements of Islamic architecture, and the Jews their own quarter (Juderia), an attractive maze of white houses and narrow, shady streets.

63.
Looking at this view of Málaga, a definition of Cubism automatically comes to mind: '... the reduction of painting to designs in space... three dimensional geometry...' Pablo Picasso, an early Cubist, was born near this town.

63

64.
A crescent moon on a window decoration in Alicante hints at a Moorish past which is annually revived in the mock battles between Moors and Christians in outfits of the period.

64

65.
The village of Setenil lies off the
beaten track, untouched by the
twentieth century, northeast of Cadiz.

66.
Gypsy tribes are thought to have
reached the Iberian peninsula in the
early fifteenth century. This group of
children near Almería are among the
estimated 800,000 gypsies now living
in Spain.

66

67

67.
Casares (Málaga) is one of the many
small towns along the Costa del Sol
transformed by the year-round influx
of holidaymakers. The area is also
popular with North European
expatriates.

68.
Under the hands of Moorish masons, even a watermill like this one on the Guadalquivir took on a fortified appearance. The control of water and waterways was essential in medieval Spain, with all the implications for agriculture, transport, power, and even life itself.

68

69.
Andalucía is a summer home for many species of birds: vulture, golden eagle, peregrine and warblers, among others. The flamingo with its long legs and vermillion plumage is the most easily identified, and least disturbed, by amateur ornithologists.

69

70.
Houses near Málaga, and all around
the Mediterranean, are painted white
to deflect heat and for other good
reasons. They demonstrate the truth
of G.K.Chesterton's observation that
'White is not a mere absence of color;
it is a shining and affirmative thing, as
fierce as red, as definite as black'.

70

71.
A house built into
rock in the village of
Setenil (Cadiz), one
of many curious small
places in this region.

71

72

74.
Segovia is shaped like a flat-iron. At
the tip, parting two streams, is the
Alcázar, the fortress-palace begun in
the thirteenth century by Alphonso VI
of Castile. ▶

75.
In the nineteenth century, every
European capital wanted to acquire
some monument in the style of ancient
Egypt. The obelisks and sphinxes that
proliferated in public places had often
been carried off as spoils by
archaeologists or generals. The temple
of Debod in Madrid, by contrast, was
saved from the area flooded by the
building of the Aswan Dam and given
to Spain by the Egyptian government. ▶ ▶

72.
A combination of rocky ground and
the wish to inter members of a family
together led to this unusual cemetery
in Málaga, where the problem was
solved by building upwards instead of
excavating graves.

73

73.
A shrine at Montoro near Córdoba, a
city that was for nearly 500 years a
great center of Islamic culture, the seat
of a caliphate renowned for its wealth,
learning and literature, and for its
3000 mosques.

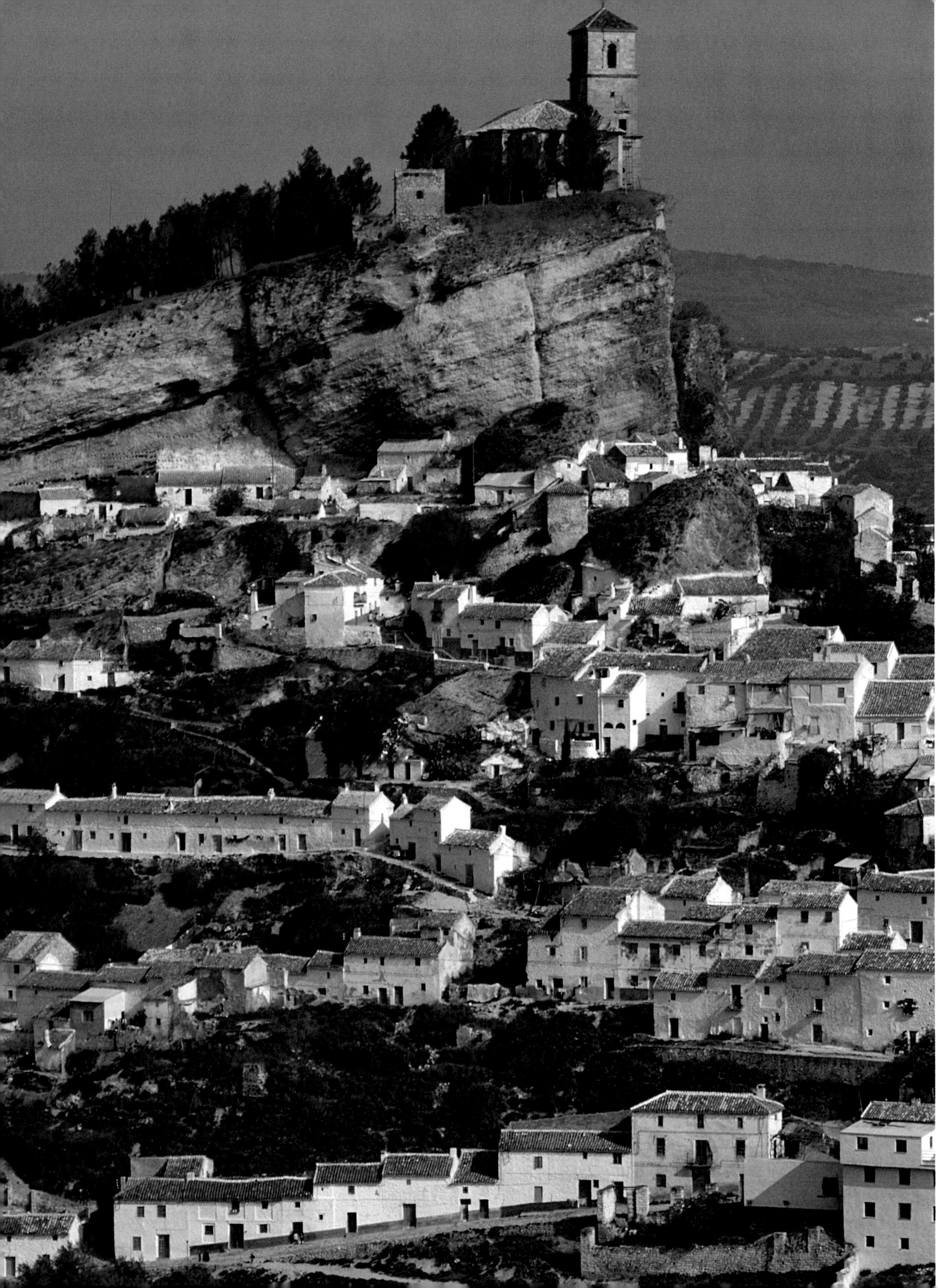

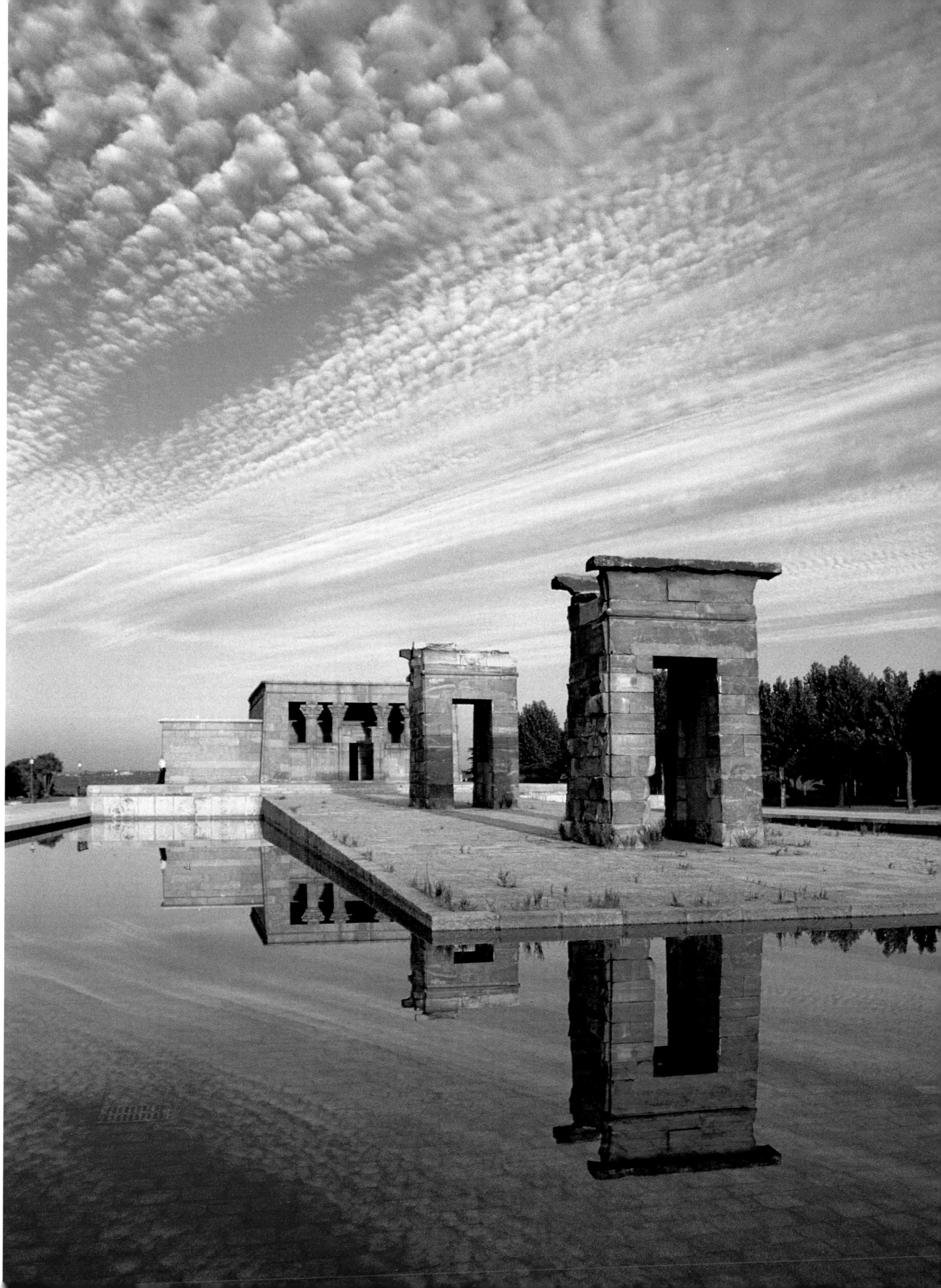

76.
The oldest known paintings were
discovered only a century or so ago on
the roofs of caves at Altamira in
northern Spain. These lifelike
depictions of bison, boar and other
beasts, first noticed by the explorer's
young daughter, were delineated some
14,000 years ago by Cro-Magnon
cave-dwellers.

77

77.
The hill of the Cruz de los Cuatro
Postes at Ávila offers a fine view of
the Adaja river and surrounding
countryside.

79

79.
The genius of Roman
engineers is best seen
at Córdoba, Mérida,
Alcántara, and here
in Salamanca, where
the Punte Romano
crosses the Tormes.

78

78.
The walls of Ávila, built at the end of
the eleventh century, are astonishingly
well preserved. The city is the burial
place of Tomas de Torquemada (1420-
1498), the Dominican prior who
became Inquisitor-General. During
his 15 years in office, some 2000
persons were burned as heretics and
many thousands more mutilated.

80

80.
Ampurias, a few miles south of the
French border on the Costa Brava, is
the site of a Greek settlement of
around 500 B.C. and a superimposed
Roman town of 209 B.C. It has
yielded many valuable finds, some in
the Archaeological Museum in
Barcelona.

81.
Castles sprang up all over Christian
Spain as feudal lords created places of
refuge from Moorish incursions. The
walls of Ávila, with 88 cylindrical
towers and nine gates, were
constructed in the late eleventh
century, after which the city was never
again taken by the Moors.

81

82.
Benbarre (Huesca),
where this castle
stands, is a small
town not far from
Lérida. It was near
here that Julius
Caesar defeated
Pompey's generals in
49 B.C. in the stuggle
for control of the
Roman state.

82

83.
Towerhouse of the Duke of Infatado at Medoza, close to Vitoria, (Álava), the scene of a famous battle (1813) when the Duke of Wellington defeated French forces and Joseph Bonaparte fled, leaving behind paintings he had carried off from the royal collection in Madrid. Thesé now grace the walls of the Wellington Museum in London.

84.
The great chateau of Riofrio, 55 miles from Madrid, built for Isabel Farnese, widow of Philip V, commands a magnificent view of the Castilian plateau. An ambitious woman who had dominated her husband, she was not surprisingly exiled from court when her stepson ascended the throne. ▶

texts, marks the emergence of Spain into written history. The Phoenicians founded Gadir (modern Cadiz), a highly civilised mercantile center. A century or so later they were followed by the Greeks, who traded all along the Mediterranean seaboard. Herodotus records that Greek traders from Samos had reached Tartessos by 700 B.C.

While the Iberians were busy in the south, from over the Pyrenees in the seventh and sixth centuries B.C. came the comparatively less advanced Celts, who had no method of writing, no sculpture, painting or coinage, and left nothing behind that approaches the gravely beautiful 'Lady of Elche', a remarkable stone bust by an Iberian sculptor of the fifth century B.C. (now in the Archaeological Museum, Madrid). The Celts did, however, blend well, and when the two major influences met, they combined, somewhere near present-day Burgos, according to Roman accounts of the Celtiberian tribes. Today, Galicia, though, is still accounted part of the European 'Celtic fringe'.

The Phoenicians' loss of Tyre to the Assyrians led to the rise of their powerful North African colony, Carthage, as the major trading power in the Mediterranean, and a head-on conflict with another ambitious city-state, Rome. Hannibal, best known of all Carthaginians, besieged and took the Spanish city of Saguntum (modern Sagunto), a Roman ally, whereupon Rome declared war (219 B.C.). The Second Punic War was one of the great touch-and-go conflicts with enormous implications for mankind. Spain supplied the silver and mercenaries with which Hannibal crossed both the Pyrenees and the Alps to ravage central Italy, but never to conquer Rome itself. While the Carthaginians pillaged in Italy, Scipio Africanus, a general of genius, began the Roman conquest of Spain in 218 B.C. All Carthaginians were expelled in 206 B.C., but for almost two centuries the Romans had to fight on to subdue the stubborn tribes.

Spain was a frontier where a succession of ambitious Romans served, hoping to earn promotion and a reputation. Cato (whose phrase "*Delenda est Carthago*" — Carthage must be destroyed — was fulfilled in 146 B.C. when the city was razed and the site ploughed), Pompey, Julius Caesar and Augustus all commanded in Spain, pushing inland against bitter resistance. Roman civil wars also had an unsettling effect when consuls in Spain became too independent of Rome. The rich, urbanised south of Spain was relatively easy to romanise, the rest of the peninsula was hard going. Pliny the Elder called Spaniards "an obscure people with barbaric names". All the same Spain provided four of the best emperors: Trajan, Hadrian, Marcus Aurelius and Theodosius, as well as distinguished writers such as Lucan, both Senecas, Martial and Quintillian, who, perhaps sensitive to Roman criticism, obligingly romanised their names.

From the Roman conquest the country gained roads, bridges, aqueducts and, most significantly, a national administration. Rome took soldiers, metals, food and taxes. There were large-scale uprisings by tribes such as the Celtiberians and the Lusitanians (inhabiting Portugal and the middle of Spain), but Roman rule was steadily expanded. It was Augustus who suppressed the last vestiges of native resistance, in the northwest corner, in 19 B.C.

There now followed a long period of peace for Hispania, as the Romans called their colony, during which Spain became one of the richest, most cultured and governable of the provinces. Only one legion, the Seventh Gemina (Legio VII Gemina), quartered in León, was permanently stationed in the country. The extension of Roman citizenship played a crucial part in the settling period that followed the conquest, though it was not until Vespasian (A.D. 74) that an edict granted the rights of the empire to all Spaniards. It is at least likely that around A.D. 63 to 67 a balding, determined Roman citizen, St. Paul, visited Spain before returning to his death during the persecution of Christians by Nero.

The onset of the Roman twilight in Spain was marked by incursions across the Pyreness by Teutons and Franks. The country was invaded by the Vandals under Gaiseric, who crushed the remains of Roman authority before accepting the surrender of the territory by a treaty in 435. Gaiseric pushed on, gained control of the western Mediterranean and sacked Rome in 455; Spain, providentially, did not detain him for long.

It was the Arian Christian Visigoths, sharing with the Hispano-Roman peoples they conquered an awareness of Roman social and political organisation, who showed a willingness to settle. Greatly outnumbered by the peoples of their colony, the Germanic Visigoths wielded military power, which they flexed unhesitatingly against each other while attempting to suppress rebellions in Galicia and among the Basques. The main impediment to the integration of Visigoths and Hispano-Roman peoples was the fact that the former were Arian Christians while the subjugated but influential Roman nobility was orthodox. Arianism rejected the concept of the Trinity and argued that the Son was neither equal to the Father nor eternal. With the conversion of the Visigoth king, Reccared, to the Catholic faith of the majority of his people at a public ceremony in Toledo (589), the irksome religious tension was reduced.

The next century saw the steadily growing domination of the Church over the king and government. In the meantime, Muslim Arab expansion had begun at the other end of the Mediterranean and reached Spain along the North African coast by the early eighth century. Factional disputes were a traditional feature of the election of a Visigoth king, and those in 710 were no exception. Bitter rivalry drove one thwarted family to invite Arabs to come to their aid. An Arab general, Jabal-Tariq, disembarked at a point later named after him, Mount of Tariq (Gibraltar). At the head of 7000 men, he defeated the Visigoths, killed their king, Roderick (Rodrigo), and pursued the survivors to a conclusive victory at Mérida. Despite their defeat by a Visigoth force at Covadonga in 718, the Moors pressed forward into France until routed by the Frankish leader, Charles Martel, at Poitiers in 732. The defeat not only averted the religious war that threatened Europe, it sent the Moors trailing back to rule the people who had invited them into Europe in the first place.

The Moors in Spain: 756-1492

Facing the Moorish army on its return from the debâcle at the hands of the Franks was a country bitterly divided. The Moors themselves brought no political unity, one immediate reason being the need to allocate the spoils of the country they had conquered. Another was the seething political struggle in Damascus, where the successors of Muhammed, the Umayyads, were overthrown by the rival tribe of the Abbasids, bringing confusion and divided loyalties throughout the Arab empire. One man who escaped the triumphant Abbasids was Abd-ar-Rahman, a member of the Umayyad family. He fled to Córdoba where he successfully established an emirate independent of Damascus. Córdoba flourished under his rule, as did other cities such as Seville, Málaga and Granada, for the Moors were essentially a townspeople who developed thriving centers for commerce and for industries involving wool, glass, metal and leather. They also encouraged the growing of fruit and vegetables, some new to Spain. They introduced the study of astronomy and the use of Arabic numerals, which paved the way for improved mathematics in a manner unlikely if clumsy Roman numerals had been retained.

The Moors respected the thoughtful man. Averroës (1126-1198) was a lawyer and physician of Córdoba who became more influential among Jews and Christians than among fellow Arabs, by whom, for a time, he was banished for suspected heresy, having proved a bit too thoughtful. An interpreter of Aristotle, he attempted to reconcile religion with philosophy, though he considered freedom to speculate should be confined to the philosopher, while the uneducated man should devote himself entirely to the Koran. The contribution of the Moors to Europe permeated medicine, science, mathematics, learning and language. In Spain, however, the greatest Moorish heritage is their brilliant architecture, which in many ways reflected the extraordinary sophistication of their culture.

After a thirty-year struggle to impose order on *al-Andalus*, as Moorish Spain was called, Abd-ar-Rahman's determination to create in the far west of the Islamic world a society to rival Damascus was ultimately successful. A remarkably refined civilisation evolved, in which religous toleration removed all the potential for trouble existing among Christians, Moslems, Jews, Spaniards, Berbers and Arabs. Christians living in Arab society were known as *Mozarabs* and treated with respect. Some of them prospered and like the Jews had their own quarters in the cities. There were, however, many Christian converts to Islam.

The Great Mosque in Córdoba, founded in 786 and much enlarged over the next two centuries, is a wonderful architectural expression of Moorish opulence, combining air, light, color and geometric patterns into a shrine of enduring elegance. Because they were a desert people by origin and the Koran enjoined daily cleansing, the Arabs not only irrigated land for horticulture, they added baths, ponds and waterfalls to their villas and gardens. Water and greenery often established the oasis-like mood of ease that characterises so many Moorish ambiences.

During the tenth century there are signs of change. In 929 Abd-ar-Rahman III turned the emirate into the caliphate of Córdoba by proclaiming himself 'Caliph and Commander of the Faithful', an act which made Córdoba equal with all other Muslim realms. In 976 a boy caliph succeeded, but all effective power was firmly grasped by Al-Mansur (the Victorious), chief minister and virtual ruler from 981 until his death in 1002. Perhaps he expressed the mood of the time, or he may have needed to distract attention from this usurpation of authority; either way, he undertook with unprecedented brutality a series of aggressive campaigns against the Christian princes of the north. Christian captives now labored on the extension of the Córdoba mosque after Al-Mansur sacked Barcelona, attacked León, Coimbra and Burgos, destroyed the church of St. James at Compostella and had the bells and doors transported to the Great Mosque by slaves. Christian envoys had offered tribute and homage to Al-Mansur, who led fifty-seven expeditions against them before his death.

His rule not only left the peninsula in a state of war between the caliphate and the five Christian kingdoms of Spain: Asturias, León, Navarre, Aragón and Catalonia, but dissensions of Al-Mansur's making among the Moors. These were sufficient for Count Ramon Borrell of Barcelona to join with rebellious Muslim forces and sack Córdoba in 1010. The Moorish solution of breaking down the caliphate into twenty-three units only made them vulnerable to Christian incursions, while the rivalries between the Christian states led to confused loyalties on all sides — as evident in the famous account of the life of El Cid. Rodrigo Díaz de Vivar was a Castilian nobleman who around 1081 switched his allegiance from the Christian King Alphonso VI to the Muslim king of Zaragoza. After several expeditions, in 1094 he finally captured Valencia, where he established himself as protector in name but in effect ruler.

In 1095 Pope Urban II launched the First Crusade to recover Jerusalem from Islam. The conflict between the spiritual and material aims of that drive to the east was reflected in Spain. Attitudes hardened as the contest increasingly became a holy war. Spanish religious nationalism maintained links with the rest of Christian Europe, above all through the pilgrimage route to Compostella, a particular channel for French influence, much of it stemming from the great monastery of Cluny. By the end of the eleventh century there had been a wholesale revision of Mozarab rites and the beliefs of dissenting Christians that was to integrate Spain with France and Rome into the one and indivisible Church. In 1086 a Cluniac monk was significantly made bishop of Toledo, although Alphonso VI, who had accepted its surrender, took the title 'Emperor of the Two Religons' to suggest his tolerance.

To conteract the advance of Christian influence, the Muslim kings now turned for help to Morocco, where Al-Mansur had established a viceroyalty. It came in the form of a fanatical Berber sect, the Almoravides, 'those vowed to God'. They brought all the ferocity of recent converts to Islam and rapidly conquered the eastern coast of Spain until checked at the gates of Barcelona. As their rule of fifty years showed signs of decline, a resurgence of Christian militancy became an invitation for another intolerant sect from Morocco, the Almohades, to bring fresh vigor to the struggle. A response came from Pope Innocent III, who called for Christians throughout Europe to join in repulsing the Almohades. Alphonso VIII of Castile led a combined Christian force to the plains of Tolosa where, in July 1212, he won a victory that destroyed organised Islamic resistance in the peninsula.

The rest of the thirteenth century is the saga of the *Reconquista*, the Reconquest. In 1236 Córdoba surrendered to the united forces of Castile and León under Ferdinand III, Valencia followed in 1238, Jaén in 1246, and after a long siege, Seville fell in 1248. By the end of the century Moorish domination of Spain had ended. Granada was the last haven of Muslim refugees from the fighting, and even Granada became a Muslim state under Christian protection.

The raising of great cathedrals — Toledo, Burgos, León, Barcelona — is a surprising feature of a century when so much effort went into warfare. Thanksgiving to God, piety, relief and employment for artisans all played a part. The synthesis of religious with military duties is to be seen in the orders of monastic knights created in the late twelfth century: Calatrava, Alcantara and Santiago. Their task was to safeguard the Christian borders, a role they shared with the powerful order of Knights Templar until these latter were disbanded as heretics by decree of Pope Clement V in 1305.

The necessity for Christian and Muslim to coexist dwindled in the

Artist's impression of the islands discovered by Columbus on his first voyage, engraving illustrating the letter sent by Columbus to Sánchez.

The port of
Genoa, Columbus'
native city, wood-
engraving from
the Supplementum
Chronicarum by
Giacomo Foresti,
1486.

aftermath of the defeat of the Almoravides and Almohades. The *Mudéjars*, Muslims living in areas under Christian domination, were allowed their own religion and customs, in the way that the *Mozarabs* under Islamic rule had retained theirs, but those in towns were restricted in their rights, while the rural population was exploited and heavily taxed. Their plight was generally ignored by the rulers, who were preoccupied by partisan politics and perpetual feuding, all of which delayed the reunification of Spain.

Two states loomed above all others in the struggle for power. Aragón capitalised upon the trading affiliations of Barcelona, taking control of Catalonia and Valencia, and building up a commercial empire which included Sicily, Sardinia and parts of Greece. Castile occupied Murcia and Alméira, but also acquired territories overseas, including the small kingdom of Naples. The strength of Castile was not in its economy, which relied heavily on tribute from the Moorish kingdom of Granada. Wealth grew out of land-grabbing, privilege and the accumulation of honors and influence. Many of the great estates were located on harsh terrain where agriculture was difficult. A solution was found in sheep farming, which in turn led to the creation of the crown-chartered sheep-owners' guild. Their flocks grazed all over the country and supplied Europe with much of its wool.

Union — the alternative was continuing war and rivalry — came about when the yearning for peace brought together Ferdinand of Aragón (1452-1516) and Isabella of Castile (1451-1504). Although they were married in 1469, real political unification did not come about until 1479 and the settlement of a dispute over Isabella's right to the Castilian throne. Their reign marks the beginning of Spain's modern history. Obedience to the crown was established and internal disputes reduced, if not eliminated.

When Ferdinand died, twelve years after his queen, the Spain he left behind was an Atlantic power and the chief rival to France and England. The monarchs who achieved this remarkable feat complemented each other admirably. Both were intelligent, experienced and had a united aim; she supplied the flair while he provided the steady, shrewd statecraft which allowed them to build on their achievements. Their first undertaking was the completion of the Reconquest. In the 1480s one Arab town after another toppled before the Christian forces: Ronda was taken in 1485, Málaga in 1487. The fall of Granada in 1492 signaled the conclusion of the Reconquest. On January 2 of that year, the keys of the city were personally handed over to the 'Catholic Monarchs', who promised to respect Islamic tradition. Later, when the remaining Moors complained that the promise had not been kept and rebelled (1501), they were faced with conversion or expulsion.

They should not have been surprised, for the Jews had been expelled less than a decade earlier, albeit by different administrative means. In pursuit of religious unity, Ferdinand and Isabella obtained in 1475 a papal bull from Sixtus IV to found the Sacred Office of the Holy Inquisition in order to convert Jews to Christianity. Aragón had its own Inquisition, but under the new papal bull the first Inquisitor-General, Tomás de Torquemada, exercised authority in both Aragón and Castile, unlike Ferdinand and Isabella, who ruled only their own kingdoms and maintained their own traditions within them. Their union was one of crowns, not kingdoms. To the crowns was now joined the Inquisitor-General, and we see the cross, in whose name unity was forged, become the crown's guardian and counsellor. It is not uncommon in unstable societies to probe people's beliefs and ideas. In Spain this process, intended to establish the religious and public status of converted Jews, degenerated into ferocious bigotry. The Inquisition became a racist persecutor rather than a religious tribunal, a means of calling into question people's faith, confiscating their possessions at best, and torturing or burning at worst. Either way, the Spanish Inquisition exercised enormous power until its abolition in 1820. For example, it examined St. Igantius of Loyala and St. Theresa of Ávila for heresy, and sometimes banned books approved by the Holy See. In March 1492, the Inquisitor was charged with responsibility for the expulsion of all Jews who refused baptism. Those who left, some 170,000, went to North Africa, Greece or Turkey. Those who remained were required to show evidence of their true conversion and lived in constant fear of being denounced. In the long run, the expulsion of the Jews and the repression of the converts who stayed amounted to the elimination of a capitalist middle class which could have played a vital role in the economic future of the country.

That economic future was closely linked to Christopher Colombus, a Genoese who had settled in Lisbon in 1477 and, working in the sugar trade, unsuccessfully attempted to secure support for a voyage to the west. King John II of Portugal found his demands excessive: Columbus wanted the title 'Admiral of the Ocean', the Viceregency and hereditary rights of government over the territories he would find, and a tenth of all profits. Rebuffed, Columbus transferred his supplication to the court of Spain, where he spent eight years seeking the support of Ferdinand and Isabella. Hardly had they entered the Alhambra than Columbus pressed once more for an interview, at which he was again turned down. However, the Church had become interested, and influence from that quarter reversed the decision.

On August 3, 1492, the Portuguese-built caravels *Pinta* and *Niña* were led out to sea from Palos by the flagship *Santa Maria*, and steered towards the Canaries. On board, in addition to the crew, were a physician, a surgeon, pilots, interpreters (one fluent in Chaldean!), a judge and a royal notary, present to record events and maintain an interest in the monarchs' portion. All that was missing was a priest. On September 6 the fleet stood out from Hierra in the Canary Islands and sailed due west. Early in the morning of October 12, a lookout, Juan Rodriguez Bermejo from Triana, shouted: "*Tierra, tierra!*", a cry that would resound around the world. At the time it must have irritated Columbus for it meant that he had lost the 10,000 maravedis (a Moorish coin used in Spain) which the queen had promised the first man to sight land. On October 27 the expedition glimpsed Cuba, and on December 5 reached Hispaniola, where the *Santa Maria* was wrecked on the north shore. Columbus hurried back to Spain to claim his title 'Admiral of the Ocean', announce his discoveries and prepare the next expedition with 17 ships and 1500 colonists.

For a navigator searching for the Indies or for the commander of a flagship that had just sunk, the end of 1492 may not have seemed all that propitious. Columbus was undoubtedly in the wrong place, but his timing, and that of his patrons, could not be faulted. It is tempting to linger on that year and upon Columbus, who was never to know with certainty that he had discovered a quarter part of the globe. He would have to plead for the acknowledgement of his rights and ended his days

85.
The fantastic church of the
Holy Family (Templo de la
Sagrada Familia) in
Barcelona, begun in 1882 and
still unfinished.

in poverty.

His visions of the land to the west which his skills as a mariner made real attracted other navigators, conquerors and fortune-hunters, not least a Florentine business representative in the commercial service of the House of Medici. Amerigo Vespucci sailed along the northern coast of South America and later made expeditions further south, down 6000 miles of unknown coastline. The businessman became a brilliant navigator who not only established a system of reckoning longitude, but calculated a figure for the earth's circumference only fifty miles short of the precise measurement. He was also quick to question that the new continent was part of Asia, and when a German geographer published a book, in 1507, referring to the New World as America, the name caught on and has retained its appeal to this day.

Spain finds and loses a New World: (1492-1830)

Queen Isabella, whose Castilian financing had backed the voyage of Columbus and others, did not survive long enough to see a major return on her inspired investment. When she died in 1504, her daughter Joanna, who had married Philip of the Austrian House of Hapsburg in 1496, became queen of Castile. Philip I (Philip the Handsome) was an ambitious young man who contested Ferdinand's rights and became joint-ruler with Joanna in 1506. In the same year he died suddenly at the age of twenty-eight leaving an inconsolable widow, who became insane and is generally referred to as 'Joanna the Mad'.

King Ferdinand's remaining years were devoted to consolidating power under the Spanish crown. Aragón held Sicily and Sardinia, and when the French showed expansionist interests in Italy, Ferdinand despatched the best of his Castilian generals of the Reconquest, Gonsalvo de Córdoba, who annexed Naples and left no doubt about the long-term intentions of the Spanish presence. In 1512 Ferdinand occupied Navarre and added it to Castile, thereby establishing boundaries for Iberian Spain which have lasted until this day. By astutely marrying his children into the royal houses of England, Austria and Portugal, Ferdinand laid the foundations for extending Spain's interests. His death in 1516 saw Spain well established in Europe, with many of his plans yet to bring returns.

If he had, by comparison with the focus of his attention upon Europe, tended to neglect the New World, the New World had not neglected him. Towards the end of September 1513, Vasco Nuñez de Balboa, a native of Jerez de los Caballeros, after an epic march through jungle, swamps and forests, had waded into the surf brandishing the Castilian flag and declaring the Pacific to be eternally a Spanish royal possession. The colony of Darien in the easternmost part of the isthmus of Panama, from which he had set out, had existed for about a decade or so before Balboa's discovery of the Pacific. His feat may have cost him his life, for his envious father-in-law, Pedrarias de Ávila, the local governor, had him beheaded on a trumped-up charge of treason, in the main square of Acla on January 12, 1517. Two years later, as if to reinforce the point of the execution, Pedrarias moved the settlement from Darien to the site of Panama City. This episode is an early illustration of the cruelty and taste for personal power which was to make unity on the other side of the ocean as difficult as ever it had been in fifteenth-century Spain.

86.
The dizzy pinnacles of the church of
the Holy Family underline Gaugin's
observation that 'Art is either
plagiarism or revolution'. There can
be no doubt regarding the direction of
Antonio Gaudi's genius.

87.
Antonio Gaudi, who took over the
construction of this vast church and
set his imprint on it, was tragically
killed by a tram in 1926 on the street
of Barcelona, a city that has some of
his finest buildings.

90.
Sitges, not far from Barcelona, is a shimmering white seaside resort. In the narrow side streets, preparations are made for the feast of Corpus Christi, when processions pass over 'alfombras', artistic carpets of flowers and foliage. ▶

91.
There is a saying in Barcelona: 'Arms and silver are of no use unless well used.' Today , antiquated weapons still have their use: as showpieces in a fiesta parade. ▶▶

88.
Gaudi's radical serpentine construction in the Guell Park, Barcelona, is appropriately sited in a town that became the center of Spanish socialism, synicalism, anarchism and other insurrectionary movements, as well as the stronghold of Catalan separatism.

89.
A window in the church of the Holy Family illustrates the seething activity characteristic of Gaudi's work, and the manner in which he drew inspiration from a wide variety of sources, blending them into a creation unmistakably his own.

92.
A flamenco artist performing in a
Barcelona restaurant displays all the
concentration, dignity and
temperament typical of this musical
form. The guitar is a later innovation
in flamenco, which in its early days
was accompanied only by hand-
clapping.

93.
On first hearing, the rhythm, cadence
and chromatics of the flamenco seem
strange and hard to follow, yet few
listeners can be unmoved by the
passion, power and skill of the
performers.

94.
What could be more impermanent in
art than the work of the pavement
artist? Perhaps this is part of its
universal appeal.

95

95.
Lord Byron, always forthright in his opinion, was rather harsh about Spanish art: '... and in Spain I did not think much of Murillo and Velazquez.' One wonders what he would have made of Picasso, Miro or Dali. This Barcelona art student, demonstrating her skill on the sidewalk, may one day join the long list of celebrated Spanish painters.

98.
The ancient craft of weaving is still
carried on in Barcelona, often among
families who have a long tradition of
working hand looms.

96

96.
Where better than a park bench in
Barcelona for an exchange of those
confidences which mark the transition
from child to adult the world over?

97

97.
With France only a faw miles distant,
it is no surprise to find the girls of
Barcelona resemble their northern
cousins in chic and poise.

99.
A benign climate like that of Barcelona enables everyone to spend a large proportion of their time out of doors.

100.
Not so long ago, public displays of affection would have been heavily frowned upon. Social change in Spain has been more dramatic than anywhere else in Western Europe.

100

102.
High upon his monument in Barcelona, Christopher Columbus points the way his dreams led him and Spain would follow. Thanks to the farsighted patronage of the Spanish queen, this Genoese navigator helped to make the Spanish crown master of half the New World. ▶

101.
Even domestic animals observe the time-honored custom of the siesta, the afternoon nap for which Spanish has provided the perfect name.

Charles I, one of the towering figures of Spanish history, arrived at Santander from Flanders in 1517, assumed the throne after securing the abdication of this mother, Joanna the Mad, and then had her confined for the remaining forty years of her life. An unattractive young man who spoke no Spanish, he inherited from Ferdinand Aragón, Castile, Granada, Naples, Sicily, Sardinia and Spanish America, to add to his own possessions in the Netherlands, Luxemburg and France. When his grandfather Maximilian died in 1519, Charles I was elected Holy Roman Emperor as Charles V. The election involved bribery on a large scale, and much of the Spanish treasury went to the German electors. This fact, combined with the constant presence of his close group of Flemish advisers, who were indifferent to Spanish interests, did nothing to endear him to his people early in his reign.

The situation deteriorated when Charles levied taxes on the mainstay of his support, the nobles and the Church. When he departed for Germany to be crowned Holy Roman Emperor, the cities of Old Castile, full of resentment against a monarch who imposed high taxes, ignored their advice and spoke no Castilian, rebelled. Charles was threatened with a reinstatement of his mother, Joanna the Mad, and popular demands that all matters relating to the welfare of the state should be discussed. For a time the Spanish nobility wavered, but increasing unrest on their own estates, coupled with the King's agreement to reduce their taxes, finally won them over. The nobles joined with Charles's foreign troops and at the battle of Villalar in 1521, the rebels were crushed and their leaders executed.

Although Charles V spent only sixteen of the forty years of his reign in the peninsula, he learned Castilian and gradually won the respect of his Spanish subjects, who may not have admired his obsession with Hapsburg imperialism at the expense of the bullion coming from the Americas, but supported his stand against the Protestant movement, in which their national religious zeal was at one with his own. Comparable zeal kept Spain involved in interminable and financially draining wars abroad. By virtue of being Holy Roman Emperor, Charles V fought the Protestant German princes and the Turks, encroaching through the Balkans into Austria. He fought four wars in France and financed a mercenary army in Italy against Pope Clement VII, which led to Lutherans sacking Rome. None of this military effort was to Spain's lasting benefit. On the contrary, the cost of dispatching armies all over Europe consumed the gold and silver coming from America.

Spain experienced rising prices and higher taxes, and became economically weak and unproductive. Too much of the trans-Atlantic riches which did not finance pointless military campaigns was invested in unprofitable estates or gold and jewelry for the nobles. There was also the Church, whose estates in Spain were vast and expanding. The same Church which championed the war of the Reconquest, now sent priests to the Indies for the support of the colonists and the conversion of the natives. Less successful were Spanish priests in Charles's European wars, where they encountered the new spirit of the Reformation.

Another financial obligation Charles V faced rested with Augsburg financiers, the firm Fugger, who had been helpful when Charles bribed the electors for the title of Holy Roman Emperor. The Fuggers opened up branch offices in Spain in order to assist in the disposal of the supplies of New World bullion discharged at the Seville quaysides. Had he had

Jewish advisers alert to the proper handling of fortunes, Spain might have benefited more than she did. As it was, Charles's aims were clear-cut; wars in Europe and the promulgation of the faith were his priorities. As a result, Castilian nobles increasingly assumed a leading position in affairs of state.

In 1554 Charles gave Naples and Milan to his son Philip, whom he married to Queen Mary of England. Two years later, old, wearied by his exertions, perhaps disappointed that he had not more to show for his long reign, Charles retired to the remote monastery of San Jeronimo in Yuste, a hundred or so miles west of Madrid. To his brother, Ferdinand, Charles bequeathed the empire — the Holy Roman Empire of the German nation — which had been too expensive for Spain and would now drain others.

Philip II, contrasted with his hyper-active father, was withdrawn, reflective and a born bureaucrat, fascinated by the administration of affairs of state. His accession in 1558 began badly with the death of his wife, Queen Mary of England. Mary, the daughter of Henry VIII and Catherine of Aragón, was a devout Catholic with a mind of her own. She watched the dramas of her father's reign unfold and inherited the crown, although a woman, single and a Catholic at heart. In need of a consort and an heir, she asked the Spanish ambassador for help in finding a bridegroom, and Philip of Spain, recently widowed, whose fervent religious orthodoxy matched her own, seemed an excellent choice. The prospect caused uprisings in Britain, but plans for matrimony went ahead. In Winchester cathedral in July 1554, Philip and Mary were married; he was twenty-seven and she eleven years older. Their honeymoon was spent at Hampton Court where Mary went the following May, believing she was pregnant, but in fact manifesting early signs of dropsy.

Philip's disappointment with this childless marriage increased when Parliament refused him a crown and the title of King of England. Eager to please her often absentee husband, Mary took England into a war against France as Spain's ally; the disastrous outcome was the fall of Calais in January 1558 and the loss of England's last possession on the continent. Her death not only loosened the ties with Spain, but allowed the accession of her Protestant half-sister, Elizabeth I, who would become an arch-enemy.

By the time Philip II was enthroned, Spain's European ambitions had waned measured against the crucial importance of her New World possessions. To Seville came ever greater volumes of treasure accompanied by legends of the Seven Cities of Gold, the Amazons, and El Dorado, which suggested that even more fabulous riches were there for the taking. The conqueror of Mexico, Hernán Cortés, more than anyone embodies the extraordinary courage, resourcefulness and ruthlessness of the times. With several voyages already behind him, Cortés commanded an expedition to Mexico in 1519. With the help of a female slave Maliche — baptised Marina — who spoke Maya and Aztec, he learned that the breathtaking Aztec empire was riddled with discord. Like so many conquistadores, Cortés regarded the New World as a place in which to carry further the Reconquest. To this task he brought energy, leadership and fanaticism which seemed the true mark of religion. He also brought the same high-handedness, jealousy and taste for personal glory that made unity in his homeland a recurring problem.

With his band of adventurers, soldiers, navigators and monks, Cortés set off for Tenochtitlan, first scuttling his ships so that the only way was forward. Montezuma, ruler of the Aztec empire, greeted Cortés as a descendant of Quetzalcoatl, the feathered serpent god of the Aztecs, which enabled the Spaniard to take him hostage and rule through him. Cortés was embroiled in fights with fellow Spaniards as well as Aztecs, in one of which Montezuma was killed. On August 13, 1521, after a three-month siege, the capital fell, and with it the Aztec empire and the social and cultural organisation of the Indians in Mexico. The later career of Cortés followed a chequered pattern. Charles V made him a marquis but refused him the governorship of Mexico, and after a series of quarrels with other nobles Cortés sought justice unsuccessfully in Spain, where he died neglected in 1547.

The pattern of the conquest of Mexico was followed a decade later by Francisco Pizarro in Peru. After a twenty-year apprenticeship in the Indies, as the Spanish called the New World, in 1531 he sailed from Panama, scaled the Andes and, declaring friendship, seized Atahualpa, the Inca king. Atahualpa offered a room full of gold as a ransom, which was accepted, but repaid with execution on the grounds of plotting against both his brother and Spanish sovereignty. The conquest of Peru followed rapidly, as well as the allocation of land and riches. Pizarro's greed, ambition and ruthlessness was exceptional even by prevailing conquistador standards. In a fitting end to a career marred by treachery, he was murdered over dinner by a rival faction in 1541.

Far away in the mid-Pacific, in 1521, Magellan had discovered some islands which were named after the infant Philip, later Philip II, in 1542. The Philippines' conquest did not begin until 1564 and Manila was not established until 1571. But the islands had less easy booty to offer, they had no central administration like the Aztecs or Incas, and the rise of Manila as a trading center in the Far East was to be both slow and closely studied by the envious trading companies of the Dutch and British.

More pressing problems faced Philip II closer to home. Despite the treasure floating into Seville, Spain became increasingly indebted to foreign banks, and its own commerce was declining. Spain's Catholicism, buttressed by the Inquisition, became steadfastly gloomy and threatened by the growing popularity of the Protestant faith. In 1567 Philip appointed the Duke of Alba to govern in the Netherlands, with firm instructions to put an end to growing disorder. This provoked William the Silent, who had served Philip II as a diplomat, into raising an army to drive the Spanish forces out of the Netherlands. Although unsuccessful at first, William's cause attracted a great deal of support at home and abroad, and the foundations of Dutch independence were laid before his murder at the hands of a French Catholic fanatic in 1584.

Earlier, in 1571, the fleet of the Holy League commanded by Philip II's brother, Don John of Austria, defeated the Turkish fleet at Lepanto near Corinth. It was a victory in which the whole of Europe could rejoice as some 10,000 Christian galley slaves were released and the threat of Ottoman predominance in the Mediterranean was removed.

The menace from northern Europe remained and Philip II's attention was brought back to England when Mary, Queen of Scots, a Catholic sympathetic to both the Papacy and Spain, was accused of plotting against Elizabeth I and beheaded in 1587. In her will, Mary favored Philip as a claimant to the English throne, disinheriting her son in the process. Raids by English privateers were openly encouraged by Elizabeth I, and Philip's fleet which was fitting out in 1587 in Cadiz was raided by Sir Francis Drake, who also attacked a Spanish squadron off Cape St. Vincent. Outraged by a queen who usurped his legitimate claim to a throne, protected the pirates who fired on his galleons, oppressed English Catholics, supported rebellion in the Netherlands and executed his cousin, Mary, Queen of Scots, Philip prepared to invade England.

Convinced that God was on the side of Catholics, he planned in meticulous detail for a Spanish fleet, under the Duke of Medina Sidonia, to sail to Flanders. From there it was to convoy the army of the Duke of Parma to England as a prelude to the seizure of the throne for Philip. The Armada consisted of about 130 ships and carried 30,000 men. Delays occurred before leaving Lisbon in May, continued off northern Spain, and it was July before the formidable fleet entered the Channel to find the Duke of Parma was not immediately ready to embark upon the invasion. The English fleet made incessant attacks upon the galleons, sent in fire ships after the Armada had anchored for the night in Calais Roads, and when the Spanish ships were driven northward by the wind next day, the threat was over. The Armada made its anxious way home around the north of Scotland and the west coast of Ireland, with tumbling Atlantic seas on the one hand and inhospitable shores on the other. Only half the fleet returned home, which was the signal to impose a new tax on Castile.

Philip settled even deeper into his huge granite palace to reflect upon God and whether He had forsaken the Catholic cause that had been a vital part of all Philip had attempted. He continued to drive himself relentlessly in his workroom, giving himself to the minutest detail of the destiny of his still substantial empire, suspicious of those around him and, although a patron of the arts, living an austere life. Philip never perceived that the empire over which he exerted sovereign rule was the Reconquest continued, a military- and Church-inspired speculation for individualist adventurers, nobles, priests and courtiers rather than a political and economic enterprise for pioneers, frontiersmen and businessmen who recognised the paramountcy of the collective state. There was no lack of courage, faith or resourcefulness; missing was the willingness to change a once successful prescription for the Reconquest and to recognise the potency of the changes taking place in Europe.

It is difficult not to feel some sympathy for the physically afflicted and mentally exhausted, four-times-married Philip. Some comfort may have come from the death of King Sebastian of Portugal fighting in Morocco in 1578. Philip prudently would not finance the expedition and the eager Sebastian, who combined a Jesuit upbringing with a sickly constitution, plunged his army and himself into a battle in which the army was annihilated and he was killed. The crown passed to Sebastian's uncle, who died in 1580. Portugal then passed to Philip, bringing the Iberian peninsula under one monarch for the first time.

Philip died in 1598 to be succeeded by the twenty-year-old son of his marriage with Anne of Austria. Philip III reigned over a kingdom embracing Spain, Portugal, Flanders and southern Italy, as well as the Americas from California to Cape Horn but — maybe wisely — declined to rule his inheritance. Confining himself to staunch Catholicism and the pursuit of pleasure, he appointed the Duke of Lerma as his premier and left virtually all matters of state to him. Lerma advised Philip to expel the Valencian Moors (1609), to the ruination of the area, which

Isabel (Elizabeth) of Bourbon, first wife of Philip IV.

148

was hard hit by the departure of these skilled farmers. In their place came new landowners, such as Lerma and his cronies, who enriched themselves by the confiscation of Moorish property. The peace agreed with the English in 1604 and with the Dutch in 1609 marked a significant Spanish withdrawal from Europe and from overseas territories. Lerma was made a cardinal shortly before his excessive venality led to his downfall in 1618 and to the return of some of his recently acquired estates.

In 1621 Philip III died. His reign had seen decline in trade and agriculture, while grandees gathered ever larger properties and assets into their hands. Like the aristocracy, the Church, holding title to some 9,000 monasteries, seemed little affected by the down-turn in national prosperity. Culturally, Spain was amazingly lively, producing the talents of Cervantes, Lope de Vega, El Greco and Zurbarán — all the more amazing as the Inquisition, relentlessly pursuing heretics and expanding its web of informers and spies, kept all intellectual and cultural matters as well as religious issues securely in its grasp. Across the Atlantic, the Indian population had dwindled to about one million, three percent of the number when Columbus landed.

When Philip IV inherited the throne, he adopted the practice of appointing a premier and leaving him to run the state, devoting himself instead to patronage of the arts. He made a much better choice of chief minister than his father by selecting the honest, energetic, but unsuccessful, Gaspar Olivares. This was the time of the threadbare grandeur of Don Quixote. Olivares, who had gained an early influence over the king, threw himself into ridding the court of corruption and strengthening the central government in Castile. Hard as he fought for reform, he never solved the crucial problem of finance which kept Spain on the verge of collapse. Nor did he prevent the country from being drawn even more deeply into the Thirty Years' War, fought mainly in Germany. Although Spanish troops, unpaid and ill-equipped, sustained their nation's reputation by their stubborn courage, Spain gained nothing from her involvement. The mid-1620s were some of the better years of Philip IV and Olivares. They could boast of 300,000 infantry and cavalry in their pay, 500,000 militia under arms and 108 men-of-war at sea, an army in Flanders and another in Bavaria, employed against France, England, Sweden, Venice, Savoy, Denmark and Holland among others. The boast meant that all bullion from the New World was no sooner landed in Seville than it was collected to repay debts or debt interest and the current costs of maintaining the enormous war machine. A check to this machine and to Spanish pride came in 1628 when in a brilliant coup, the Dutch Atlantic fleet fell upon the silver fleet in Cuba and carried off all of the treasure. The Spanish admiral responsible was tried and later executed in Cadiz. It was not only the loss of revenue that mattered; the worth of the galleons and the ordnance was three times greater than the value of the cargo.

Revenues from the New World declined in the 1630s, leading to the imposition of unpopular new taxes at home, the bulk of which were borne by Castile. In an attempt to solve Spain's chronic financial problems, Olivares proposed a more equitable distribution of the tax burdens throughout the empire. The result was the confrontation with the three *Cortes* (parliament) of Aragón, Catalonia and Valencia. France came to the aid of the Catalans, turning a rebellion at arms into a conflict that ended with the Peace of the Pyrenees (1659), a humiliating treaty for Spain marking the end of her role as a supreme power in Europe.

In 1640, the throne of Portugal, which had so effortlessly moved to Spain sixty years earlier, was claimed by the Duke of Braganza, who was crowned as John IV in Lisbon. Philip stubbornly contested this usurpation of his sovereignty, but had neither the financial means nor popular backing to wage an effective war. Recognition of Portugal's independence finally came in 1668.

Olivares was driven out of office in 1643 and died a broken man in 1645. Philip IV resolved not to leave state affairs in the hands of others and to take a more personal interest. In effect he clung to the idea of kingship as a sacred trust and while only too well aware of the cost, nevertheless challenged the French, Dutch and English on land and at sea, entering into wars which were politically and financially disastrous. When he died in 1665, he left behind him a nation physically and spiritually exhausted as well as a society still given to consumption rather than production.

Hardly surprisingly, the fortunes of Spain did not improve when Philip was succeeded by his four-year-old son, Charles II, a sickly sufferer of chronic ill-health. The last of the inbred Hapsburgs to ascend the Spanish throne, he was first cousin to his mother, Mariana of Austria, the daughter of Philip's sister. She became regent and continued in the role after Charles reached his majority, by which time there could be no doubt he was mentally sub-normal. He married twice but he had no children. Given his disorders, that may have been a merciful intervention of providence, but the question of the succession was obviously a dilemma awaiting its day. Mariana, a pious woman, turned for advice to the aristocracy and the Church, which led to their enrichment (the Church numbered 180,000 employees by the 1660s) and the auction of high posts, even those of viceroy of Mexico and Peru.

Mariana's incompetence bought a threat from Don Juan (Juan José) of Austria, the illegitimate son of Philip IV and an actress. The prince had fought in Naples, served as viceroy in Sicily and was sent in 1566 to command in the Netherlands. There he lost the battle of the Dunes in 1658 against the French near Dunkirk, and was summoned back to Madrid. Charles II attained his majority, aged fourteen, in 1675 but, unsurprisingly, exerted no influence on the government of Spain, which became steadily more corrupt. In 1677, with substantial backing from friends and the army, Don Juan marched from Aragón to Madrid, seized power, banished the queen mother and assumed leadership without deposing the king.

It was one thing to seize power, quite another to implement reforms which by now the whole country agreed were vital. Don Juan had little time to follow up his coup, for he died in 1679. Perhaps the very poverty of Spain only excited the rapaciousness of those with responsibility for government. It may be that no one with insight could see the possibility of bringing about reforms that would effect improvement in his lifetime. The administration was as impotent as Charles II, who spent his last years in a dream, suffering convulsions, dominated by his second wife and surrounded by his priests, clairvoyants and physicians. He died in 1700, having willed the throne to Philip, Duke of Anjou, a grandson of his elder sister, Marie Thérèse, and Louis XIV of France.

The eighteenth century which brought the Enlightenment to Western Europe and to America was to make but slow progress in Spain. Sparked by Isaac Newton's discovery of the fundamental universal order, the early champions of the Enlightenment sought to popularise a rationalistic and scientific approach to religious, social, political and economic issues. Under attack came feudalism, dogmatism, censorship, reliance on authority in spiritual or scientific matters, bigotry and restrictions upon trade or trading enterprise. There was no common program, but the confrontation of ideas was meant to change attitudes and involved many great names of the century: Descartes, Locke, Diderot, Franklin, Paine, Voltaire, Rousseau, Pope, Kant and so many others. Alas for Spain, the import of a Bourbon brought little by way of enlightenment from any quarter, and the Spanish clergy and aristocracy, who saw immediately the threat to their privileges, were implacably opposed to foreign heresies.

Some kind of agreement on the Spanish succession had been — far-sightedly — reached by England and France about two years before Charles II died. Unfortunately the agreed candidate died first, which caused confusion as to which one, of four candidates, would best suit the interests of England, France, the Netherlands, Austria etc. Louis XIV encouraged a pro-French faction in Spain to designate his grandson as sole heir to the throne and triggered the War of Spanish Succession (1701-1714).

Despite the name, the major battles were fought outside Spain. In a nutshell, the war was an alliance of England, Holland and most of the German states against France, Spain, Bavaria, Portugal and Savoy. The Duke of Marlborough and Price Eugene of Savoy, who after being refused a commission in the French army by Louis XIV — a refusal the king would come to regret — became one of the great commanders of his time, won the famous battles of Blenheim, Ramillies, Oudenarde and Malplaquet. By the ensuing Peace of Utrecht (1713), Philip of Anjou was to be recognised as king of Spain, but France renounced all rights to the Spanish throne, razed fortifications at Dunkirk, and handed over Newfoundland to England. Spain ceded Gibraltar and Menorca to England and Sicily to Savoy, while Austria acquired Naples, Milan and the Spanish Netherlands.

The Prado, Madrid, in the reign of Philip IV, engraving in the Municipal Museum, Madrid.

103.
Little remains to indicate that Frias (Burgos province) was once a frontier post around which the Moorish hosts advanced and retreated, battling for occupation of this picturesque little town.

Philip V's reign did not begin well. Because Catalonia, Aragón and Valencia had sided with the claim of his chief rival, Archduke Charles of Austria, Philip removed most of their autonomous privileges as a punishment. As a Bourbon he encouraged the cause of the Enlightenment and with French advisers campaigned to reduce the power of the Church so as to increase the authority of the state. Dominant at his court in Madrid was the remarkable Princess Marie Ursins, a French noblewoman and diplomat, who arranged Philip's marriages, defied Louis XIV, insisted on Spanish independence from France and exerted virtually dictatorial powers. Philip tended to be dominated by women. His Italian second wife, Elizabeth Farnese, encouraged Philip to regain Spanish territories in Italy and managed to have the Princess Ursins banished — small gratitude for the fact the princess had arranged her royal marriage.

For all Philip's extravagance in building palaces — La Granja (or Little Versailles) at San Ildefonso, the Royal Palace in Madrid, the Aranjuez, among many — it was during his reign that the economy began to stabilise, industry started developing in Catalonia, and the progress engendered elsewhere by the Enlightenment began to filter into Spain. In fact, Spain's success brought it into the conflict which closed his reign. The master of an English ship, Robert Jenkins, claimed that Spanish coastguards had severed his ear, and when his ear was displayed in Parliament, England declared war. The hostilities which followed were really a conflict between the commercial interests of England and Spain, the former eager to establish trading links within the vast overseas dominions of the latter.

Philip V died in 1756 to be succeeded by his son Ferdinand VI, then aged thirty-four. His father's attempts to release the stranglehold on the national economy were continued in the hands of Ferdinand's hardworking chief minister, the Marquis of Ensenada, who sought to maintain peace while alert to the need for a strong navy, if the overseas possessions were to be retained. His economic and fiscal reforms began to show signs of success, which made his enemies nervous and, inevitably, intrigues against him finally brought about his dismissal.

Charles III had been an able king of Naples for twenty-four years when he succeeded his half-brother, Ferdinand, on the Spanish throne in 1759. His devout Catholicism did not stop him from dealing firmly with the Church; he dismissed the Inquisitor-General for drafting a bill without prior royal permission and went on to banish the Jesuits (already expelled from France and Portugal) for political intriguing. He made his ministers answerable to the crown and never hesitated to dismiss anyone who failed to meet his standards. Charles not only managed to keep Spain out of the worst of the wars, he also picked the winning side, and for his support of the American colonists in the American Revolution, he regained Florida in 1783.

Devoted to the interests of Spain, Charles encouraged the advancement of well-educated nobles and administrators. As a believer in free trade, he broke the monopoly of Cadiz and Seville so that American trade was legitimised through all Spain's major ports, a development which encouraged her re-emergence as a superior maritime power. Charles III could not solve all the problems of years of neglect and deeply vested interests, but he did demonstrate what could be done and displayed an authoritative zeal which manifested itself in most of the areas delineated by the Enlightenment. Spain prospered under a Bourbon king who brought his

104.

Vineyards in La Rioja have a history going back at least to the twelfth century. Long used to fortify other wines, their product has increasingly earned an international reputation in its own right. ▶

105.
Although mechanisation has eased the labor of viticulture, it is still true that 'the best fertilizer is the farmer's foot' and a bent back the augury of a good harvest.

106.
The sheer physical toil of wine-making is forgotten when a striking pose memorably captures a way of life little changed by twentienth-century innovations.

106

156

107.
Grape pickers enjoy a picnic lunch in
the Longroño district of La Rioja,
which takes its name from the Rio
Oja, a tributary of the Ebro.

108.
The severity of expression caught by so many celebrated Spanish portrait painters is still to be encountered in rural regions, always with a shock of recognition.

108

112.
A winter reverie of austere church and resting vineyards captures the season when nature slumbers and the wine-grower enjoys a well-earned rest. The church is Santa Maria de la Piscina near Logroño (La Rioja).

113.
Santander is a popular holiday resort but also has to work for its living. Fishing vessels ply along the coast and further out in the shallow but treacherous waters of the Bay of Biscay.

114.
Restaurants all over Spain testify to the riches to be found in Spanish waters: sardines, mackerel, cod, bonito and the occasional swordfish. Here fishermen of the Cadiz area, near Cape Trafalgar, encircle tuna in their nets. ▸

115.
Pontevedra (Galicia), where these gulls quarrel, has many claims to fame, not least the fact that Columbus' caravel, the 'Santa Maria', was built locally. ▸▸

116.
The Cantabrian coast has any number of delightful little fishing villages and ports where visitors can try the regional specialty, fish baked in pastry.

116

117.
A fisherman spruces up his boat in Huelva, a pleasant port close to the Portuguese frontier on the Gulf of Cadiz.

117

119.
Mending nets is the eternal preoccupation of the fisherman when ashore. Stringent regulations set by the European Community fishing authorities govern methods and quotas in this industry. ▶

118.
The Mediterranean can be stormy, but the image that its name brings to mind is of a calm azure sea sparkling in the sunlight. In such an idyllic setting, the risks run by fishermen are easily forgotten.

country out of European isolation and pointed a way into the future. In the twenty-nine years of his reign he set in train an economic revival essential if Spain was not to lose trade with the American colonies; he improved the administration within the colonies and appointed Spanish administrators less self-seeking than any of their predecessors.

His failure, if judged as such, was to pass the throne in 1788 into the hands of his ineffectual son, Charles IV, who was to leave control of the government in the care of his queen, Maria Luisa, a domineering, dissolute consort. In 1793 she appointed Manuel de Godoy, a court favorite and her lover, as chief minister and heaped honors upon him — dukedoms as well as posts of general and admiral. When Louis XVI was guillotined in the same year, his nephew Charles IV was appalled by the prospects for himself and declared war on France, a move that brought French armies into Catalonia and the possibility of a republican revolt. Godoy made peace with France in 1796 and invaded Portugal in 1801.

With the Napoleonic Wars in full swing, in 1805 he entered into a disastrous alliance with France which resulted in the Combined Fleets of France and Spain setting sail from Cadiz, in late October 1805. Off Cape Trafalgar, in a relative calm before a storm, the Combined Fleets, unfamiliar with operating together, were pitched into a battle against a single well-trained fleet commanded by Vice-Admiral Nelson, a seaman of genius. The flagship of the Spanish commander was the *Santissima Trinidad*, the biggest and most powerful man-of-war afloat. After hours of battle, she was boarded and taken with over 400 dead on board. So badly battered was her hull that she foundered in the gale which followed the engagement. Spanish marine pride sank with the *Santissima Trinidad* beneath the grim cold waters of the Atlantic, no further than 20 miles from her own coastline.

The defeat of Trafalgar only added to Godoy's unpopularity, driving him to attempt a deal with Napoleon, who had lost confidence in Spain as an ally. A revolt in Aranjuez in 1808 by Spaniards disgruntled with Godoy compelled the abdication of Charles IV in favor of his son, Ferdinand, who had been intriguing against him. This gave Napoleon the opportunity he needed. He summoned Charles and Ferdinand to Bayonne, presented them with papers for their abdication, and offered the throne to his brother, Joseph. Charles IV and his family, beforehand so pitilessly portrayed by Goya, were imprisoned in France. This act, along with the occupation of Spain by French troops, led to uprisings against Joseph, who was proclaimed king in Madrid in 1808. This was the last straw. Popular resistance was instantaneous and widespread. Within three months of ascending the throne, Joseph was forced to leave the capital.

Before the end of the year, Napoleon personally arrived in Spain at the head of an army of 200,000 men and within a year was in control of the whole peninsula. But the emperor had underestimated the national pride and fighting spirit of the Spanish people. Guerillas continued to fight smaller French garrisons and impede communications and supplies. So promising was the revolt, England sent an expedition under a talented general with experience in India, Sir Arthur Wellesley (later Duke of Wellington). In six years of mobile warfare Wellington both extricated his forces resourcefully and won a series of victories, reaching Toulouse by April 12, 1814, when news of Napoleon's abdication arrived.

Two years previously, a group of patriots in Cadiz had drafted a Constitution designed to prevent the rule of favorites and limit the monarchy. When Ferdinand VII was restored to the throne in 1814, he refused to be bound by it. Liberals rose in arms, but Louis XVIII sent French troops, and supporters of the liberal cause had to disappear or go into exile. Spain was again riven with dissension, but this time there were to be far wider consequences than before. The first quarter of the nineteenth century saw the emancipation of almost all Spanish possessions in America. A combination of the ideals of French republicanism, the North American example and the events in Europe and Spain, encouraged rebellion and the creation of independent states in most of the colonies. After the battle of Ayacucho in 1824, of the great empire on which the sun never set, only the islands of Cuba, Puerto Rico and the Philippines remained.

The years of French occupation of the motherland meant there was little to be done to prevent the secession, and in any case the question of an heir to the throne, the familiar Spanish preoccupation at home, was beginning to draw affairs of state toward another crisis.

Spain finds itself: 1830 to the present day

The end of the Peninsular War and restoration of Ferdinand VII did not bring a new dawn. Dissatisfaction with his regime caused conservatives to despair of his policy of keeping the country apart from developments in Europe, and to consider the advantages of replacing Ferdinand by Don Carlos, his even more reactionary brother. Affairs came to a head soon after childless Ferdinand married his fourth wife, Maria Cristina, in Naples in 1830. She was twenty-four and he, although only forty-six, was in poor health. On Fedinand's death in September 1833, Maria Cristina astutely arranged for their infant daughter Isabella to be proclaimed queen, with herself as regent, though the right of female succession to the throne was hotly disputed.

The First Carlist War immediately broke out, liberals supporting the cause of Isabella, while the Church, reactionaries and Basques championed Don Carlos. The liberal supporters of Maria Cristina believed in constitutional government and in particular in the Constitution of 1812. Maria Cristina was not personally convinced of the need for liberalism, but had no alternative power base. The Carlists' reactionary and clericalist attitudes gave what began as a dynastic dispute a strongly political character. The war was increasingly notable for extreme cruelty on both sides, neither seeming capable of gaining a lasting and final victory over the other. In 1837 the Carlist army reached the outskirts of Madrid but was driven back to the north. By 1839, however, the Carlists were vastly outnumbered and defeated. Don Carlos escaped to France and renounced his claim to the throne in favor of his son.

The man chiefly responsible for Don Carlos' defeat was the general and statesman Baldomero Espartero, who had fought in the Peninsular War and later against the revolutionaries in South America. After the signing of a peace treaty at Vergara with the Carlist general Maroto, Espartero played an increasingly important political role. His opposition, backed by the army, forced the queen regent to resign and retire to France. Espartero established himself as regent but accomplished little that was pleasing to his supporters, despite sequestering some of the monasteries and eliminating the Inquisition. There were uprisings, including an unsuccessful attempt to seize the palace and the child queen in Madrid. Finally, in the summer of 1815, Espartero boarded a British man-of-war and departed for exile in England. He returned to Spain five years later and was to hold the posts of premier and commander-in-chief of the army after Isabella was enthroned.

Isabella II, in whose cause all the bitter and bloody fighting had taken place, was declared of age in 1843 and married her religious, hypochondriac cousin, Francisco de Asis de Bourbon, in 1846. Her right to the throne was recognised by France and England, while the claim of Don Carlos had been accepted by the Papacy, Prussia, Russia and Austria among others. Her marriage was a different matter, arousing as it did England's fears that the French would gain too great an influence in Spain. Isabella, married at sixteen, was content to be a figurehead of state. She was, however, profligate in her favors to the point of nymphomania and avaricious in the acquisition of a safe private fortune.

Though Isabella II was a frivolous figure and her government engaged in continuous dispute, her reign is distinguished by striking economic expansion. The stimulus came from the surplus capital being generated in the rest of Europe by the Industrial Revolution. Spain with its natural resources and manpower, but lacking merchant capital and expertise, seemed an excellent place for investment. Barcelona installed the first steam engine in Spain in 1834; two years earlier the first blast-furnace was brought on-steam in Marbella, and from these modest beginnings further grander schemes were developed. A Belgian company financed the expansion of the zinc industry, a British company invested in the Rio Tinto mine with the biggest copper deposit in Europe. French capital

Drawing of crowds flocking to a bullfight in Seville.

helped to build the Spanish railway network and the gas company in Barcelona, while in Pamplona it was Dutch money that financed the gas installations.

Industry driven by steam was able to move away from the water and wind-power of the past. Catalonia flourished and in the Basque country an iron industry began to develop, often fueled by British coal shipped in exchange for the iron produced. Between 1830 and 1860 mining production tripled, between 1818 and 1860 the population of Barcelona quadrupled, and in 1855 Barcelona had its first general strike. Agriculture was still the mainstay of the economy: a census in 1858 records that 66 percent of the population worked on the land, whereas about eight percent were craftsmen or engaged in industry.

At a time when economic prosperity seemed feasible despite the government and monarchy, a crisis involving both coincided with a slump and an uprising against Isabella, who left for France in 1868. The leaders of the revolt, determined to find a monarch, offered the Spanish throne to a prince of the Prussian house of Hohenzollern, which fitted in with Bismark's machinations but not those of the French. Protests from France, concerned for her valuable investments in Spain, led to the throne being offered to Prince Amadeus of Savoy, and that in turn became an issue for the Franco-Prussian War of 1870-71. The repercussions of that war rumbled on until the assassination of an Austrian archduke in Sarajevo in 1914 touched off an even bigger war.

Amadeus was elected king in November 1870 and arrived in his capital in January, the month that Paris, stricken with famine, surrendered to the Prussians. It was not an auspicious inauguration. The dissensions of ministers, animosity of the army, widespread preference for a Bourbon or Don Carlos, and the unlikelihood of his survival if the popular mood for a republic increased, all contributed to his decision to abdicate in 1873. A short-lived republic was proclaimed, but anarchy ensued, with four presidents coming and going in one year. At the end of 1874 the army restored the Bourbons, in the person of Isabella's seventeen-year-old son Alphonso, educated in Austria and England.

Alphonso XII entered Madrid in triumph in 1875 and, in the astute

Philip II transferring his court to Madrid, 1561, engraving from 'The History of the City of Madrid'.

hands of Cánovas del Castillo, maintained his personal popularity until his death from consumption some ten years later. His second wife, Maria Cristina, was regent during the minority of his posthumously-born son, Alphonso XIII. The threat of anarchy had been allayed, although still in existence, notably in Catalonia. More troubling now was an echo of the cry, "America for the Americans", emanating from Cuba, where a war of independence began in 1868 and by 1870 absorbed 100,000 troops. The Peace of Zanjou (1878) deferred the inevitable outcome until 1898, when the United States would take sides. By the end of the nineteenth century, the liberals and conservatives in Madrid had accepted debate and political stratagems as a preferred alternative to civil war. Both agriculture and industry improved and all the signs of stability attracted foreign investment, just as it had earlier.

Cuba, however, was seething again. In 1895 a new revolution broke out along familiar lines; Spanish forces garrisoned the towns while insurgents tied up industry and agriculture from the countryside. The U.S. government grew anxious about the considerable American investments in Cuba and the safety of U.S. expatriates still in the country. Cánovas del Castillo was shot by an Italian anarchist in 1897 and his mature statesmanship was much missed as the crisis lurched on. In February 1898 the U.S. battleship *Maine*, dispatched to Havana for the protection of American nationals and property, was sunk by a mysterious explosion with the loss of 260 lives. A U.S. naval enquiry reported the battleship had been sunk by a Spanish mine. A Spanish enquiry reported that an accidental explosion in the forward magazine was the cause. Whatever the truth of the matter, American public opinion was outraged and the nation spoiling for a fight, with the catch phrase, "Remember the Maine", as a rallying cry. In the ensuing Spanish-American War, the Spanish fleet suffered resounding defeats, first in Manila Bay in the Philippines and then off Santiago de Cuba, while 17,000 American troops landed in Cuba. By August 1898 hostilities had ceased, and by December the Treaty of Paris had stripped Spain of almost all her colonial possessions. Cuba became independent; Puerto Rico and Guam were ceded to the United States as indemnity, and the Philippines passed to the U.S. for the payment of twenty million dollars. The dregs of the defeat were bitter indeed. The following year the Palau, Marianna (less Guam) and Caroline Islands were auctioned off to Germany for twenty-five million pesetas.

Spain, at the beginning of the nineteenth century still a world power, had by its end lost all but its North and West African territories. What illusions of grandeur were possible now? Not surprisingly, given the times, new left-wing groups — communists, socialists and syndicalists — flourished. Even anarchism, which led to the assassination of Cánovas, became popular. Basques and Catalans sought home rule or separation from the rest of Spain. The loss of Cuba seemed to presage a setback to the fragile industry based around Bilbao and Barcelona, while agriculture, always prey to fluctuations of the weather, continued to offer only hard work for a poor or uncertain return.

A group of writers, the celebrated 'Generation of '98': José Ortega y Gasset, Miguel de Unamuno, Maria del Valle-Inclan, Antonio Machado and others, took on the task of attempting to clarify contemporary attitudes and identify the issues that deserved priority. The problem facing the intellectuals was to offer something more constructive than revolt against the old discredited order of society. Alternatives were plentifully available in Europe, but they seemed not to travel well transferred to Spain, deeply rooted in tradition. Moreover there was the danger that intellectuals who spent too long without committing themselves politically would appear to be an uninvolved élite, yet their value in rising above politics would be compromised if they became partisan. Spain's search for herself, having lost the New World, was helped by the tortured introspection of the 'Generation of '98' which, at the very least, provoked thoughtful awareness of the issues, even if real solutions and actions came from elsewhere.

The industrial economy based in the Basque country and Catalonia developed a well-organised working class with a great many grievances about autonomy, language, and the voice of industry in the affairs of the country. Strikes and uprisings were firmly put down, but climaxed in 1909 during Barcelona's 'Tragic Week'. Earlier, in 1904, Spain had secretly concluded treaties with Britain and France to retain a free hand in Morocco and, in return, not to oppose British aims in Egypt. In 1909 the Spanish army experienced a reverse in Morocco which led to the government calling up reservists. In protest, workers in Barcelona organised a general strike and denounced both the government and the monarchy. Troops intended for Morocco were sent to Barcelona, where the revolt was swiftly put down as a salutary example to the rest of Spain. The use of the army brought outcries from all over Europe, led to the minister responsible being driven from office and, inevitably, provoked questions about the role of King Alphoso XIII, who had assumed the throne on coming of age in 1902.

Although Spain was not involved in the Great War (1914-1918) and the economy improved as a result, there were continuing strikes and unrest which came to a head when, in July 1921, the Spanish army was defeated and massacred in Morocco. Recriminations rocked the country until General Primo de Rivera staged a coup in 1923 and launched a campaign in Morocco which ended in victory in 1927. Two years earlier he revoked his military dictatorship, replacing it with a civil one, but continued as the sole ruler under Alphonso. A program of public works was successful; less successful were his attempts to pacify the opposition of socialists and Catalan separatists. The worldwide economic recession in 1929 increased his unpopularity. Realising he had lost the support of both the army and the king, he resigned and retired to Paris, where he died shortly after. Republican feeling ensured that the parties of the left won the municipal elections overwhelmingly, and Alphonso XIII left Spain without officially abdicating in 1931. From Rome, ten years later, a few weeks before his death, he renounced the throne in favor of his third son, Don Juan.

The Second Republic began almost as unobtrusively as Alphonso had departed. There were many ambitious pledges made by a democratic republic of the workers, who themselves provoked uprisings which were put down by a government ostensibly representing their cause. In 1933 the election of a right-wing government led to further strikes, culminating in something approaching civil revolt by the miners in Asturias. Thousands of Moorish troops and the élite of the Spanish Foreign Legion were drafted in to rescue besieged garrisons in Oviedo. Within two weeks, with heavy casualties on both sides and thousands arrested, the disturbance was put down. Revelations about financial scandals in 1935 led to the dissolution of the ruling party and fresh elections, which produced, as in 1931, a large Republican majority. However, while the electoral system may have given a sweeping victory to the Republicans, the number of votes cast for left and right was evenly balanced, without the stability the phrase implies. A series of attempted assassinations showed that parliamentary democracy was giving way to armed rule in the streets, with one round of violence following another.

In July 1936, the rising of the military in Morocco spread to garrisons in major towns on the peninsula. From the onset, and particularly in the matter of flying General Francisco Franco's soldiers from North Africa to the mainland, outside powers took sides in a civil war polarised around the Republican left and Nationalist right. Appeals by General Franco to Italy and Germany brought immediate supplies of armaments; the Western democracies ineffectually complained and encouraged volunteers to join the International Brigades, thus fueling the conflict. All the frustrations of the past ignited with the volatility of the national temperament to make the war a contest bloody enough to compare with the War of Independence or the Reconquest. The whole of Spain's gold reserves were shipped to the Soviet Union to pay for Republican arms, but the professional tactics of trained soldiers and the greater numbers gradually recruited by Franco decided the outcome. Despite quarrels among the Republican leadership, there were successes at Teruel and across the Ebro. But with the fall of Barcelona in January 1939 the worst was over. Nationalist troops occupied Madrid and organised resistance came to an end.

The Civil War, with all the confusions that preceded it, was over, and all the burning enthusiasms that had caused it were lost in its sobering aftermath. Perhaps as many as one million people were dead or had left the country, in which communications were ruined, the economy shattered, and the people both exhausted and bewildered. Spain could be of little help to the protagonists preparing for World War II, although 18,000 Spanish troops served in the Blue Division on the Russian Front until Franco withdrew them in November 1943. Otherwise, Franco sensibly kept Spain a non-belligerent, although well disposed towards fellow fascists who had so effectively responded when he needed help.

As the country's ruler for thirty-six years, Franco displayed the austere attitudes of a general who has had the mantle of a dictator placed on his shoulders. His appearance, his voice, and his lack of experience in politics were offset by a pragmatic approach to problems, a ruthless use of his authority and a clear idea of his role in Spanish history. When World War II ended in 1945, Spain, the only fascist country in Europe, was excluded from the United Nations, NATO, and the benefits of the Marshall Plan. Near famine was avoided by shipments of wheat from Argentina, a gift from Eva Peron, the wife of an army officer who became a dictator.

In 1947, Franco's mind turned to the eternal question of succession. Following a referendum, he was proclaimed head of state for his lifetime; his successor would be selected by him from the royal family. The dictator passed over Don Juan and in 1969 chose Juan Carlos, grandson of Alphonso XIII. Earlier, in 1953, Franco had signed a treaty with the U.S.A. exchanging military bases in Spain for millions of dollars in aid. This paved the way for Spain to become a member of the United Nations. Simultaneously the economy gradually began to pick up. Spain had a long way to go, it was true, but the growth rate in the 1960s was phenomenal. The income from tourism swelled annually and was swiftly channeled into the revival of industry. From the tourists themselves

120.
The sweeping beauty of the mountains of Navarre, which form the southern face of the Pyrenees, gives way to the fertile cereal-bearing plains extending to the Ebro.

Spaniards learned about the life style of the European bourgeoisie: fashions, credit cards, recreation, appliances, discos and music, for the tourist industry had to anticipate the expectations of holidaymakers.

Although Franco's achievements never overcame his reputation, he stabilised Spain, urged the creation of a dynamic economy and ensured the return of the monarchy. In 1974, aged eighty-two, his health began to deteriorate and in 1975, when he died, Juan Carlos became king. At the time Basque terrorists had stepped up their activity and the auguries were not good. Moreover, Spain was tightly bound by the National Movement and there seemed little likelihood it would surrender its authority amicably. Instead, within two years a smooth transition had been made to democracy. First a political reform bill led to universal suffrage and the legalisation of the labor unions, Socialist and Communists Parties; the National Movement was disbanded and press censorship ended.

A general election in June 1977 was won by a collective of centrist parties with 27 percent of the vote. They immediately began work on a new Constitution designed to grant autonomy to the regions by authorising locally-elected regional parliaments to deal with local affairs. Once the new Constitution was passed, fresh elections were held with results much the same as those of 1977, but this time the coalition showed signs of tension and the party chief resigned.

Spain's even course to democracy was jolted by a specter from the military past which the nation hoped had been interred with General Franco. Into Parliament on February 23, 1981, burst 300 men of the Civil Guard and army, led by a strutting, comic figure brandishing a revolver and declaring he was there to constitute a military government and eradicate terrorism. Millions of people worldwide saw the incident on television. To most watchers, bursts of fire from the automatic weapons of the guards resembled the onset rather than the eradication of terrorism. Colonel Antonio Tejero's 'invasion' of the *Cortes* was not an isolated act. In Valencia, the garrison commander deployed tanks on the streets and put all troops on full alert. It was then that Juan Carlos showed his qualities of leadership. Addressing the nation on television that evening, he left absolutely no doubt that while he was king, the crown would support democracy and not tolerate any attempt to disrupt the process. Tejero surrendered next morning and in Valencia the troops went back to their barracks. The commitment to democracy had been demonstrated at the highest level; there would be no going back. On February 27, a million Spaniards marched through Madrid in a national celebration of the triumph of democracy. Delight in the monarchy was also widespread, and into the international limelight, somewhat reluctantly, stepped the king: tall, fluent in English, French, Italian and Portuguese, yachtsman, pilot, and graduate of all three of the armed services. The monarch, Queen Sophia, two princesses: Elena and Cristina, and Prince Felipe of Asturias, rarely out of the press, project an image of caring and working for the country without wishing to run it.

Spain became a member of the European Economic Community in 1986 and was given until 1991 to remove all protectionist trade barriers. The Socialist leader, Felipe Gonzáles, in power since 1982 and the man who steered Spain into the E.E.C., was democratically re-elected in 1989. Foreign investors injected some fifty million dollars into Spain during the closing years of the 1980s, a quantifiable sign of confidence that the political, social and economic reforms would endure.

121.
Spanish women like these on Ibiza have traditionally done their full share of farm work. Now their daughters are more occupied in furthering the flourishing tourist industry on this delightful island. ▶

122.
Spaniards have long had a high reputation in equestrian skills. The Moors took Arabian and Barb horses to Spain, where they were crossed with the native stock to produce the superior horses of Spain, for which there was a great demand in other countries. ▶▶

124.
Horsehair, once used to stuff
furniture, is no longer as prized a
commodity as it used to be, but horses
still have to be groomed and clipped
for the hot summer months.

123

123.
A round-up of horses brings in mares
and foals for branding after a period
roaming free in the winter months in
the province of Pontevedra. Spanish
soldiers and settlers introduced the
horse to the Americas. Some escaped
and became the foundation stock of
the mustangs used by the Indians of
the Great Plains.

125.
A woman in Orense looks with pride
upon a heavy-headed sheaf of wheat.
Mechanisation has now reduced much
of the hard labor of harvesting, but
the old farming methods still survive
in many upland and remote places.

126

126.
Taking a cow to market, where a lot of
hard bargaining will go on before the
animal changes hands.

127.
The Picos de Europa can be snow-
streaked as late as June. Lower down
the slopes there is perfect grazing for
horses in this lovely, unspoiled region
close to the northern coast.

127

128.
'Glory be to God for dappled
things,' wrote the poet Gerard
Manley Hopkins, and went on to
cite 'the brinded cow', ignoring
the equestrian's special affection
for this coloring on a horse.

128

129

129.
In much the same style the women pilgrims of the Middle Ages would have made their way to Santiago de Compostella, perched on a mule between laden panniers that keep the animal's pace in check.

130.
Varieties of bread on sale in Santiago de Compostella. After the perils and rigors encountered along the Pilgrim's Way, such a sight would have gladdened the heart of any pious traveler, however ascetic.

131.
Throughout the world there is a recognisable pride that goes with wresting a living from a countryside subject to all the vagaries of the season.

131

132.
Ávila, where this woman sits at work, is 3700 feet above sea level, making it the highest provincial capital in Spain. St. Theresa (1515-1582), reformer of the Carmelite order, was born there. A convent now occupies the site of the house where she spent her early life.

136.
The village of Trevélez in the Alpujarra Mountains to the south of Granada is said to be the highest inhabited village in the whole of Spain, located at 5600 feet above sea level. ▶

135.
Hay is turned to be dried by the sun and later stacked in ricks, a distinctive feature of the densely populated Basque province of Vizcaya, rich in farm produce, timber and minerals.

133

133.
Buildings in the traditional rural style in the national park of Ancares (Lugo province).

134.
Spanish onions, large and delicately flavored, are an essential ingredient in many national dishes. The red are the strongest, the yellow intermediate, and the white are the mildest.

134

Being Spanish: Life, Death and Inspiration

CITIES

MADRID

Four cities: Madrid, Barcelona, Valencia and Seville, account for around one-seventh of the total population of about forty million. Since the late 1950s, between four and five million people have shifted from the agricultural regions of Andalucía, Galicia and parts of Castile to the industrial towns and tourist zones, including the Canaries and the Balearics. Rapid industrial growth has accompanied urban development and the influx into the major cities is the outcome of agricultural mechanisation as well as the Spanish economy's drive to both expand and export.

Madrid, however, is magnetic quite apart from offering employment. It is unusual in that its attractiveness is due to its style and elegance rather than the architectural grandeur which is a feature of other cities. Immediately impressive is the sweep of the boulevards, the design of the circles, the splendid relationship of the plazas, the care taken with the parks and gardens, the smartness of the stores, boutiques and restaurants, and the gusto of the *Madrileños*, who enjoy their capital. Over 1500 restaurants serve the best produce to be found from all over Spain. There are narrow alleys, intriguing bars, golf courses, swimming pools, riding schools and even windsurfing, dinghy sailing and water skiing on nearby lakes.

Theater production has taken on a new lease of life. The national drama center and the municipally-funded Teatro Español provide a repertoire of classical and modern plays by Spanish and foreign authors. Every March sees an international theater festival, and in October and November is the Madrid Autumn Festival. There are pop and rock concerts throughout the year as well as an annual jazz festival, all of which are recorded and reported upon in the weekly magazine *La Guía del Ocio*.

The fast, clean subway goes everywhere, and is cheap and efficient, though often crowded. With increasing traffic congestion it offers one of the best means of seeing as much as possible of Madrid. Central to the city is the Puerto del Sol, where ten streets converge and all distances in the nation are measured from a marker standing in front of the police headquarters. All around are impressive, built-to-last skyscrapers which suggest that new money has blended tastefully with traditional notions of the value of elegance.

Contrasting vividly with the noise and bustle, crowded streets, business, government, construction sites, large department stores and the generally hectic rhythm of Madrid's days and nights, is one of the world's greatest art galleries, the Prado. The understandable pride of Madrid and Spain, the Prado is an eighteenth-century building which was intended as a natural history museum until Ferdinand VII, a bankrupt despot, decided to become a patron of the arts and benefactor of an art museum. Over 300 paintings from various royal palaces formed the nucleus of the collection, now numbering some 3000 paintings, 4000 drawings and 400 sculptures, displayed in 94 rooms on three floors.

As impressive as the size of the Prado may be, it is to the quality of the collection that it owes its international renown. The strongly representative presence of Spanish masters is to be expected. Seeing so many works of Velázquez together invariably elevates a foreigner's view nearer to that of the many Spaniards who consider their countryman the greatest artist of all time. Most of his works have been cleaned or restored, and after seeing half of all the canvases he ever painted, it is unusual not to come away with a higher appreciation of his genius. There are 110 paintings by Goya, 34 by El Greco, and a splendid selection by Murillo, Zurbarán, Sanchez Coello, Cano, Gallego, Ribera, Ribalta and Morales.

As a reminder of Spain's commercial and dynastic ties with the Low Countries, there are the works of Rubens. After his wife died he entered the diplomatic service and in 1628 went to Spain to arrange an agreement between Philip IV and England, spending nine months in Madrid, where he got to know Velázquez and painted the royal family. Other Flemish and Dutch masters such as Van Dyke, Rembrandt, Teniers and Van der Weyden are also present, as well as the great Germans, including Dürer, Cranach and Holbein. The Italians are represented in profusion, another reminder of the imperial past, by 36 Titians, in addition to canvases by Tintoretto, Bellini, Veronese, Botticelli, Fra Angelico, Lotto, Tiepolo, Giorgione and Raphael.

To see the remarkable, and probably best-known, example of Iberian art, the visitor must leave the Prado and go to the Archaeological Museum. There, dating from the fifth or fourth century B.C. is the 'Lady of Elche', a bust dug up in 1897 near the village of that name. The unknown artist who carved the piece caught superbly an Iberian model with a strong Greek air about her. Her head-dress resembles two intricate cartwheels, her jewelry is elaborate, but she is Spanish as surely as the head of Nefertiti is Egyptian.

No great distance from the Prado is the Retiro Park, little changed from the elegant, formal garden of the Baroque era. Then its 400 acres were a favorite venue for royal diversions, plays and water pageants. Today the park provides a delightful setting for the people of Madrid to enjoy the grandeur of the gardens along with puppet shows, concerts, and all manner of spontaneous performances. In the center is the large artificial lake El Estanque where canoes and paddleboats are for hire.

Any number of museums, galleries and churches offer not only great works of art but a cool haven from the burning heat of summer or a refuge from the icy blasts of winter winds. There is, for example, the Royal Palace, which King Juan Carlos uses only for state occasions, preferring to live outside Madrid in the two-storey, red-brick Zarzuela Palace. Consequently, it is one of the few royal palaces open to the public. After the great museums, chapels, churches and cathedral, there is the Madrid of the wide boulevards and an increasingly cosmopolitan air — the city that stays up later than any in Europe, takes two-hour lunch breaks, and has an infinite variety of *tapas* bars. *Tapas* ('lids') were invented in Seville and began as little saucers of delicacies served on top of a glass. From this humble origin has evolved one of the great gastronomic inventions of our times. The bars specialise in appetisers such as pieces of spiced sausage, delectable shellfish, strips of omelette, mushrooms in garlic butter, and variously cured hams. The customer picks out what he wants as an *hors d'oeuvre* or a full-sized portion, if sufficiently tempted, and it is not uncommon to drift from one *tasca* (*tapas* bar) to another, consuming a variety of snacks before going to dinner at 10 or 11 pm.

Because of the climate, fruit and vegetables have longer seasons than in less-favored parts of Europe. As Madrid attracts so many Spaniards, it also abounds in restaurants specialising in regional cooking. It is not difficult to sample Valencian *paella*, Castilian roast suckling pig, Andalusian *gazpacho* or virtually any other dish which may originate in the kitchens of Asturias or the Basque country, Catalonia or anywhere else. There is alleged to be one bar to every one hundred *Madrileños*. As a friend of mine once remarked: "The real beauty of Madrid is that after a physically punishing day in the museums and galleries, in the evening you have to stroll no more than half a mile from Puerto del Sol to find mouth-watering dishes from all over Spain". Madrid can sometimes be a test of stamina but it offers diversions unique among Europe's capitals.

BARCELONA

As close to Marseille or Bordeaux as to Madrid, as far from Rome or Paris as Seville, Barcelona is the obvious link with Europe, a prosperous port, center for industry, and a city which delights as much in being rebellious as it does in being industrious. Don Quixote arrived there at the end of his fourth expedition, reflecting: "Barcelona... occasioned me no great pleasure, but rather much grief. I bore them the better for having seen that city". Barcelona has been the great conduit of ideas — republicanism, communism — from the north, as well as the mighty manufacturer for the south. The city is buoyant, cosmopolitan and very much on the move, driven by Catalans who are determined to keep alive their language and their cultural identity.

Barcelona was little affected by the Moors, and though wars and politics intruded, the city steadily became richer, bolder and politically more assertive than the rest of Spain. During the Civil War the Republican capital was Madrid, Valencia and finally Barcelona. Franco was particularly severe with the Catalans and, predictably, they were a persistently irritating source of opposition. Catalan, a forbidden language for forty years, is now taught in schools, published everywhere, spoken on radio and tele- vision, and increasingly used on street signs, which can make exploration baffling for foreigners. With the staging of the Summer Olympics, Barcelona is moving on from the compulsive need to preserve its integrity within Spain to a larger international arena, and one for which its delightful situation makes it admirably suited.

The Gothic Quarter (Barrio Gotico) sits on the crown of a low hill where Hamilcar Barca, father of Hannibal, founded a Carthaginian colony. Most of the major buildings were erected much later, between the thirteenth and fifteenth centuries. As the port grew in importance, so in later centuries the town developed around the harbor, leaving behind its medieval nucleus. The quarter has become a marvelously preserved and adapted exhibition of stonework, packed with cafés, taverns, restaurants and, increasingly, antique shops, art galleries and boutiques. Within the Barrio Gotico is the cathedral, begun in 1298 on the site of two earlier churches. It comes as no surprise that a city which can excel in so much can also boast of a cathedral among the finest in Spain. Not only is the Gothic cathedral itself so impressive and magnificently proportioned, there are the chapels on three of the four sides, the two octagonal bell towers, the interior cloister where geese can be seen waddling about, and the variety and quality of the sculpture and paintings. There is the crucifix worn by Don John of Austria at the battle of Lepanto in 1571, and the lovely marble tomb of St. Eulalia of Barcelona, a victim of the Emperor Diocletian in the early fourth century.

The Ramblas is the city's famous promenade, a glorious combination of newspaper kiosks, flower shops, cafés, bars and food-stalls, backed by flourishing plane trees, behind which run an enticing variety of buildings, not least the Boqueria market, where the plentiful fruits, vegetables and fish of the province glisten appetisingly amid the hustle and din of an energetic marketplace. Most of the waterfront is committed to ships and shipping, a fact that can be confirmed by riding in the aerial cable-car. However, Barcelona also provides a municipal beach with seafood restaurants in an atmosphere which has managed to retain the feel of a Mediterranean fishing town.

The Spanish village (Pueblo Español), built in 1929 for the International Exhibition, faithfully represents architectural styles from all over Spain. Arts and craft shops in the eighty buildings have items for sale produced by artisans who can be seen at work. Then there are the museums dedicated to the Catalan artists Joan Miró and Pablo Picasso, the wonderful Art Nouveau building of the Palacio de la Musica and the huge Gran Teatro del Liceo which testify to Barcelona's contribution to art, symphonic music, ballet and opera. Naturally there are also factories, chemical plants and the industrial paraphernalia which generates wealth, but the benefits of wealth are widely enjoyed, be they the rapidly expanding sporting facilities on gently sloping Montjuich, or the museums that encapsulate the past, or the 120,000-seat Camp Nou stadium of the celebrated Futbol Club Barcelona, a highly visible expression of Catalan nationalism.

Just west of the city is the highest peak in the Collserola, Tibidabo (1800 feet), a name taken from the temptation of Christ by the devil. Reached by metro, tram and funicular — getting there is half the fun — the view embracing Barcelona, the Pyrenees, Montserrat and the Mediterranean is certainly awesome.

The rebellious and the industrious are nowhere better seen in Barcelona than in the Sagrada Familia (Temple of the Holy Family), the extraordinary modern church which towers above the skyline. As if to prove that Spain had not lost all the skills that go into creating monumental buildings, this huge, intricately carved edifice was begun in the late nineteenth century. It owes most to that highly original architect Antonio Gaudí. His ingenuity is to be seen elsewhere in the city, in buildings that are immediately recognisable, breaking away from classical vertical and horizontal lines by introducing novel serpentine and undulating configurations. Born in 1852, Gaudí took over the Sagrada Familia project in 1891 and worked on it till his death, when struck by a tram, in 1926; he was buried in the crypt. The four needle-thin spires with their melting embellishments, perforations and studded ornaments seem erratic and even out-of-place in a sacred building. It is nonetheless a forceful, contentious, grandiose enterprise which will stimulate a debate extending way beyond architectural aesthetics into religion, nationalism, propaganda and extravagance for decades to come.

VALENCIA

Hans Christian Andersen was granted a travelling stipend by King Frederick VI of Denmark and in 1864 pioneered a route to Valencia that his fellow Scandinavians have been following in increasing numbers ever since. Andersen was drawn by the people, the climate, the gypsy tribes and the legends, all elements that are still emphasised by an attentive tourist industry. Only a mile and a half from the sea, Valencia lies in the middle of one of Europe's most intensively developed agricultural regions — the *huerta* — 37,000 acres of fertile fields that feed the whole country.

The city is the third largest in Spain, one of the most prosperous and, surprisingly, despite the breathtaking setting, one of the more drab. Faced with the cramping effect of great fourteenth-century walls, a hundred years ago the city authorities decided to pull them down — and have been criticised ever since. Two superb gates testify to the scale of the military fortifications which had outlived their purpose. The cathedral stands on a site previously occupied by a Roman temple, a mosque and a Christian basilica. From the steps of the Door of the Apostles, every Thursday at noon eight men in black shirts preside over any disputes concerning irrigation water on the *huerta*. Sitting on rustic seats, the water tribunes (*huertanos*) keep no records and hear no appeals. Fines are levied in medieval currency and the proceedings are conducted in the Valencian language. Among the treasures inside are paintings by Goya, a gold enamel work by Cellini and, above all, the Holy Grail.

The Holy Grail is an especial feature of medieval myth and legend. Sometimes it appears as a chalice, a cup or a dish, sometimes as a stone or cauldron into which a bleeding lance drips blood. There are many versions. English legend has it that St. Joseph of Arimathea took the chalice from the Last Supper to England, and the powerful stories of King Arthur and his court focus upon a search for this lost chalice. Spain has two legends. One deals with Parsifal, which is the format that inspired Richard Wagner. The other version has the chalice taken to Rome by St. Peter and some time in the third century sent to Spain for safekeeping. After this it was kept in various hiding places until it was lodged in Valencia in 1399, where it has stayed ever since. Of modest size (17 × 16 cm.), the cup is of agate with a jeweled base. Experts consider it to be of Roman origin and old enough to have been used in Jerusalem at the time Christ was crucified.

Spring is welcomed to Valencia by the *Fallas*, a week-long carnival from March 12 to 19. It was the custom in the Middle Ages for carpenters to make bonfires of their wood shavings on the eve of March 19, the feast of St. Joseph, patron of carpenters. From those sensible, religious observances developed one of the most grotesque fiestas in the world. Hundreds of colorful papier-maché tableaux are constructed, some thirty feet high, and all full of color, style and wit. Neighborhoods compete in preparing bigger, more humorous effigies, lampooning politicians, customs, the famous, and life generally. Then, on March 19 at midnight, tons of fireworks are detonated, and all but the finest of the papier-maché figures

Flight in a balloon made in Madrid in 1793 by Don Vicente Lunardi, engraving.

are put to the torch. The finest is pardoned from cremation and installed with its predecessors in the Fallas Museum. The *Fallas* must be one of the most extravagant celebrations of the return of Spring to be found anywhere, and as I once overhead: 'It's not as if Valencians have a hard winter, anyway'.

SEVILLE

I recall a senior diplomat advising: "Only ever volunteer to serve in countries that have olives, vines and a flourishing tourist industry". If that waggish criterion is fastidiously applied in Spain, Seville probably fits the bill better than any other city. Its olives are the best in the world and come in many varieties; although good wines are plentiful all over Spain, the sherries of Andalucía — the *finos*, the *manzanillas, amontillados, olorosos* and sweet dessert wines are unique. And as for the tourist trade art, architecture, history and romance, castanets, guitars, orange blossom and sunshine are available in abundance.

Seville is the fourth largest urban center in Spain and one that has to earn a living from local industry, of which tourism is a relatively modest part. There are the obvious tourist attractions of the vast fifteenth-century cathedral, the Giralda, the Tower of Gold, the Archives of the Indies and the Alcázar. And there is also the second most important art gallery in Spain, after the Prado. The Museum of Fine Arts is housed in what was the old Convent of Mercy, an impressive Baroque building overlooking a charming little square. This is the kind of gallery a visitor is always glad to see because the surroundings and the building are so appealing, the collection of masterpieces is almost a bonus.

The lovely Maria Luisa Park is the setting of the Archaeological Museum, which has a magnificent collection of prehistoric items, including reproductions of the splendid goldwork of the 'Treasure of Carambolo', as well as Roman finds from Itálica. For all its rich parade of the past, Seville has been progressive and unafraid of change; Maria Luisa Park is a good example. In 1928 the city staged an Hispano-American exhibition, and as if to prove the old skills of the Moorish gardeners had survived, an area to the southeast of the city was turned into a splendid expanse of gardens and grand boulevards. The center is the Maria Luisa Park, a quarter of a mile or so of luxuriant palms, unfurling chestnuts, orange trees, casuarinas, colorful flower beds and paths linking hidden bowers, occasional ponds and shady grottos. Spain sets high standards for its gardens, but I doubt if this park is matched in Europe, let alone within Spain.

Patio is a Spanish word, and whether or not the concept originated in Seville is not as important as the use to which the patio is put. The traditional Sevillan ambience — the cool confined alleyways, shady patios, delicate wrought-iron gates, whitewashed walls and carefully tended hanging baskets, window boxes and clay pots of flowers — has a special appeal, contrasting as it does with the grandeur of the historical buildings. The popular dwelling owes a lot to the Moorish tradition. Rooms are arranged around an interior patio, sometimes open to the sky or, if roofed, decorated with plants of some kind. This colorful space may be used as a living room, somewhere for the family to meet, talk, watch television, welcome friends and relax. Inevitably, the patio becomes the focus for the household, an area combining house and garden which gives the feel of outdoors with the convenience of not being overlooked. It can be as intricate, attractive or luxurious as money and inclination permit. Every year Seville, like other Andalusian towns, holds a competition for the most beautiful patio so as to keep alive interest and reward the most skillful practitioners of the art of gracious living in a hot climate.

Flamenco, another special feature, is a traditional kind of Andalusian singing or dancing, newly created every day by each artist, and achieving an extraordinary unity of words, music, movement and feelings. Emotion is the essential ingredient, be it strange or violent, full of sorrow or alive with joy. Most people respond intuitively, whether or not they understand the words. The music, the rhythm, the dance, the costume, owe their origin, it is said, to Byzantine liturgical chants and Arab and Hebrew melodies. Many of its finest performers are gypsies.

To many foreigners and Spaniards, Seville is synonomous with fiestas. There are three that stand out above the dozens held in the city. Two weeks after Easter is the April Fair or *Feria*, one of the biggest street parties in the world, a release from modern industry and an overwhelming celebration of local good fortune. The *Feria* began as a cattle market in the mid-nineteenth century, but wine, song and dance were soon introduced and the occasion is partly a parade of horses, fashions, prowess and possessions during the day, partly an opportunity to gather so as to eat, drink and be entertained in the evening. For five days everything becomes a spectacle. There is a huge fairground, a corrida, and flamenco everywhere.

Holy Week (*La Semana Santa*) follows after Palm Sunday and sees another transformation of the city. Fifty-five brotherhoods, primarily religious organisations responsible for a variety of welfare and charitable activities, emerge from their churches and advance in dazzling processions to and from the cathedral. Beautifully-made floats are carried through the streets, together with insignia, church regalia and relics in a visually bewildering yet highly organised spectacle.

The third great festival is that of Corpus Christi. In the morning the monumental silver monstrance, the vessel in which the consecrated host is exposed for adoration, is paraded through the streets, and in the afternoons of the week young boys dressed in sixteenth-century costumes dance and sing praises to Christ and the Virgin Mary. There is not the levity of the *Feria*, or the gilded flamboyance of Holy Week, rather a more spiritual reminder of the spiritual significance of Christianity.

COUNTRYSIDE

From Santillana del Mar in Cantabria in the north to the small coastal villages of Andalucía in the south, there are hundreds of small places which capture some especial quality of the region and form part of the national heritage. The shift of population from countryside to towns left in its wake the need to preserve the former and to tackle the problems of pollution in the latter. Considerable progress has been made with environmental improvement in cities such as Madrid, Barcelona and Bilbao, while preservation and enjoyment of the countryside has been promoted by the creation of Spain's nine national parks. In this way, areas of outstanding natural beauty and their wildlife and flora are being safeguarded for future generations.

Some 600 species of Spanish fauna, many the casualties of civilisation encroaching on their territory, are believed to be at risk. The brown bear (*Ursus arctos*), male specimens of which can weigh well over 600 pounds, numbers no more than 100 or so. The Iberian lynx (*Linx pardina*) has a predominantly golden coat with black patches and is a woodland hunter thinly scattered over Castile-León, Estremadura and Andalucía. There may be 400 in existence. Pyrenean ibex (*Capra pyrenaica*) are found, if you are lucky, in the Aragonese Pyrenees, where no more than 30 are thought to survive. A bird unique to Spain is the Imperial eagle. In 1986 only 104 pairs were recorded, but strict protection in recent years is thought to have been effective and their number is increasing.

The largest national park (173,000 acres) in Europe is the Donaña, 60 miles southwest of Seville. Since the park is also the largest area in Europe without roads, the only way to see the dunes, beaches and marshes which give way to one ecosystem after another is to go with the organised tours. Visitors are not allowed on their own, to safeguard the many endangered species found here, among them about a quarter of all the known Imperial eagles. Conducted tours also have the advantage that guides familiar with the species, their movements, feeding habits and behavioral patterns are able to show the visitor more than he could ever hope to spot on his own. There are hundreds of animal species here: lynx, boar, mongoose, along with dozens of different snakes and hundreds of kinds of birds, ranging from flamingos and kites to bee-eaters and nightingales.

Some 125 miles east of the Donaña Park is the national reserve in the Alpujarras, a mountainous area south of Granada which stretches in the direction of the spas and the Costa del Sol. This is an isolated place, with wild rugged scenery, soil which is being eroded, villages that are sparsely populated, and subsistence farming as the chief means of livelihood. So far, Spain's increasing prosperity has passed by such places, but they are likely to be increasingly singled out by the more intrepid vacationer seeking the solitary Spain of the rustic past, and in the case of the village of Trevélez, a sample of ham cured in the dry air at over 5000 feet.

At the other end of Spain, on the Aragón border with France, is the superb Ordesa National Park. Nearer to Lourdes than Huesca, the park has been a protected area since 1918, allowing rhododendrons, raspberries and strawberries to grow wild, and mountain goat, boar, chamois and fox to avoid extinction. The Tres Sorores (Three Sisters) provide a triple crown of peaks rising to around 10,000 feet. From them and similar slopes more than a dozen waterfalls cascade toward the Rio Arazus valley. Torla is a gaunt, stone-walled and grey-slate-roofed village from which amblers and serious hikers can stroll or stride through scenery likely to take away any breath left from the exertion.

The future of the 'typical' Spanish village with its whitewashed walls and peasants astride donkeys is bound up with the massive migrations of workers to the towns. Over the past two decades Spain has become a nation transformed from cottage to city-dwellers. Testimony of this are half-deserted villages with empty, increasingly dilapidated houses. It is at least possible that after the whirlwind of change there will be a fresh assessment of the benefits of living away from urban centers, and the attractions of remote, unspoiled landscapes will exert the same pull as in other industrial countries. An imaginative beginning was made in the summer of 1989 when some 150 students from Scandinavia, France,

138.
Veneration of the Virgin
Mary has played an
important role in Christian
religious observances ever
since the Council of Ephesus
in 431. This statue of the
Virgin and Child is a detail of
a portal of León cathedral.

139.
Stained glass, one of the
glories of Gothic architecture,
is nowhere more splendidly
represented than in León
cathedral, perhaps the
loveliest in Spain.

139

141.
Painted arches span the tombs of eleven kings and twelve queens in the twelfth-century church of St. Isidore in León, a town founded in A.D. 68 as a camp for the Roman 7th Legion.

141

140.
St. Isidore of Seville (c. 560-636) was a learned churchman and powerful bishop who helped stamp out Arianism among the Visigoths. His relics were taken to León in 1063 and entombed in the basilica of St. Isidore, of which these Romanesque cloisters form a part.

143.
The Portico de la Gloria from the
mid-thirteenth century once formed
the main entrance of the Colegiata in
Toro but is now enclosed by the ruins
of a later, since demolished church.

142

142.
The Colegiata or Santa Maria la
Mayor in the small town of Toro near
Zamoro (León and Castile), dating
from the eleventh to thirteenth
centuries, is considered one of the
finest Romanesque churches in all
Spain.

144

144.
El Greco lived for 39 years in Toledo. Some of his finest works hang in the cathedral, built between 1226 and 1492.

145.
Alphonso VI of Castile and León acquired Cuenca as a dowry when he married the Moorish princess Zaida in 1091. He was 60 at the time, and had spent much of his life fighting his bride's countrymen. Cuenca cathedral, begun in the late twelfth century, was founded by Alphonso VII.

146.
Burgos cathedral houses the tomb of
Rodrigo Diaz de Vivar, El Cid, the
legendary soldier-of-fortune who was
exiled to Valencia by Alphonso VI of
Castile and León. It was only in 1921
that his remains and those of this wife,
Ximena, found their present resting
place. ▶

147.
Burgos cathedral, begun in the
thirteenth century, is not only
imposing from the outside, but a
treasury of carvings, paintings and
stained glass within. ▶ ▶

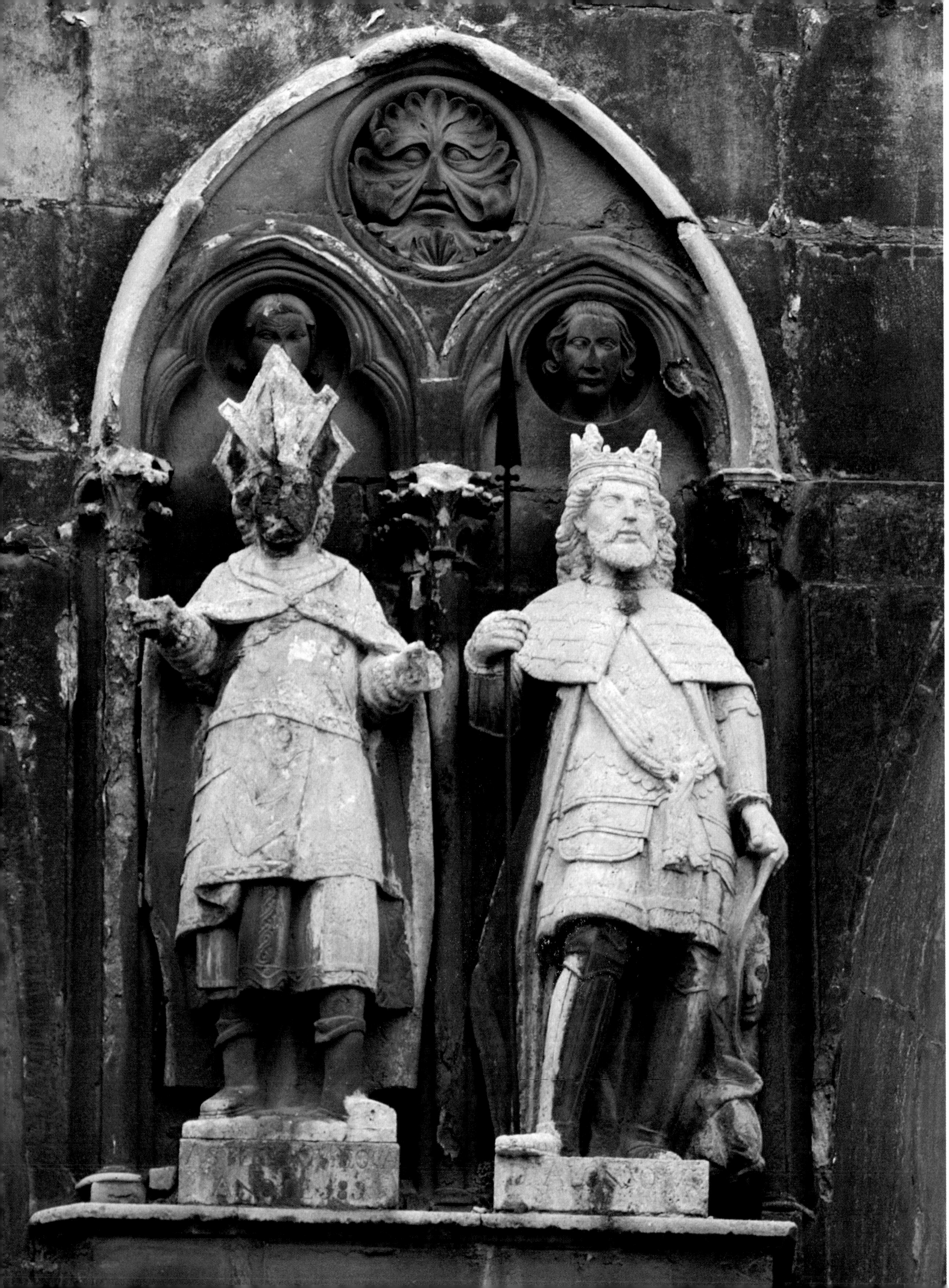

150.
Seville's fifteenth-century cathedral is the biggest in Spain, and third largest in the world, after St. Peter's, Rome, and St. Paul's London. On the same two-acre site stands the famous Giralda tower. ▸

151.
The fourteenth-century church of St. Mary in Castro Urdiales, a charming little fishing town in Santander province. ▸▸

148

148.
Segovia cathedral, one of the last great Gothic churches to be built in Spain, was begun in 1525 but not completed until the eighteenth century. This ancient Castilian city was founded by the Romans, who left behind their massive aqueduct.

149.
The vast cathedral of St. James in Santiago de Compostella, Europe's greatest center of pilgrimage in the Middle Ages. The west front, dating from the mid-eighteenth century, is a masterpiece of the exaggerated Spanish Baroque style known as Churrigueresque (after the architect José Churriguera). The fabric of the building is mostly twelfth century.

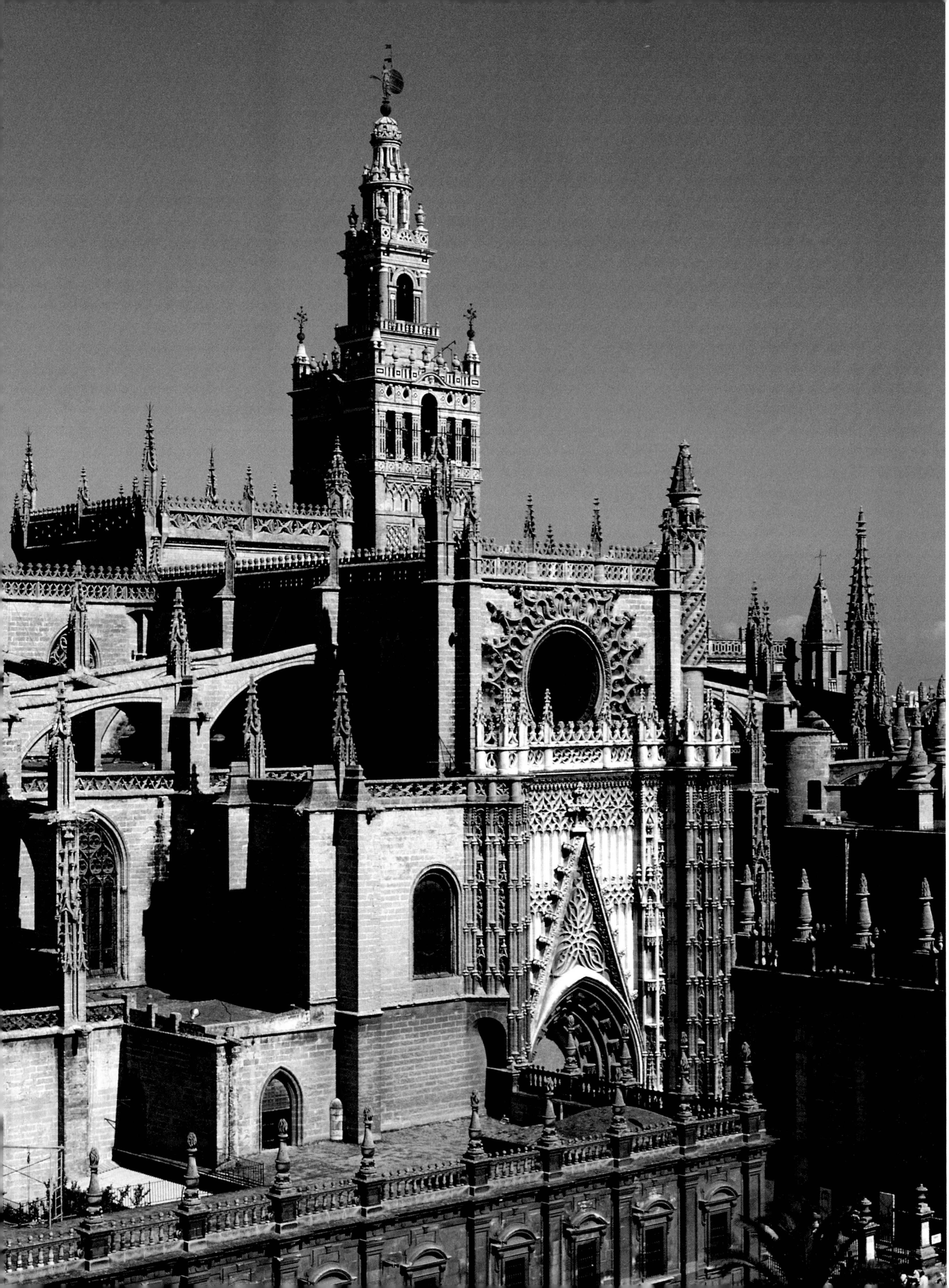

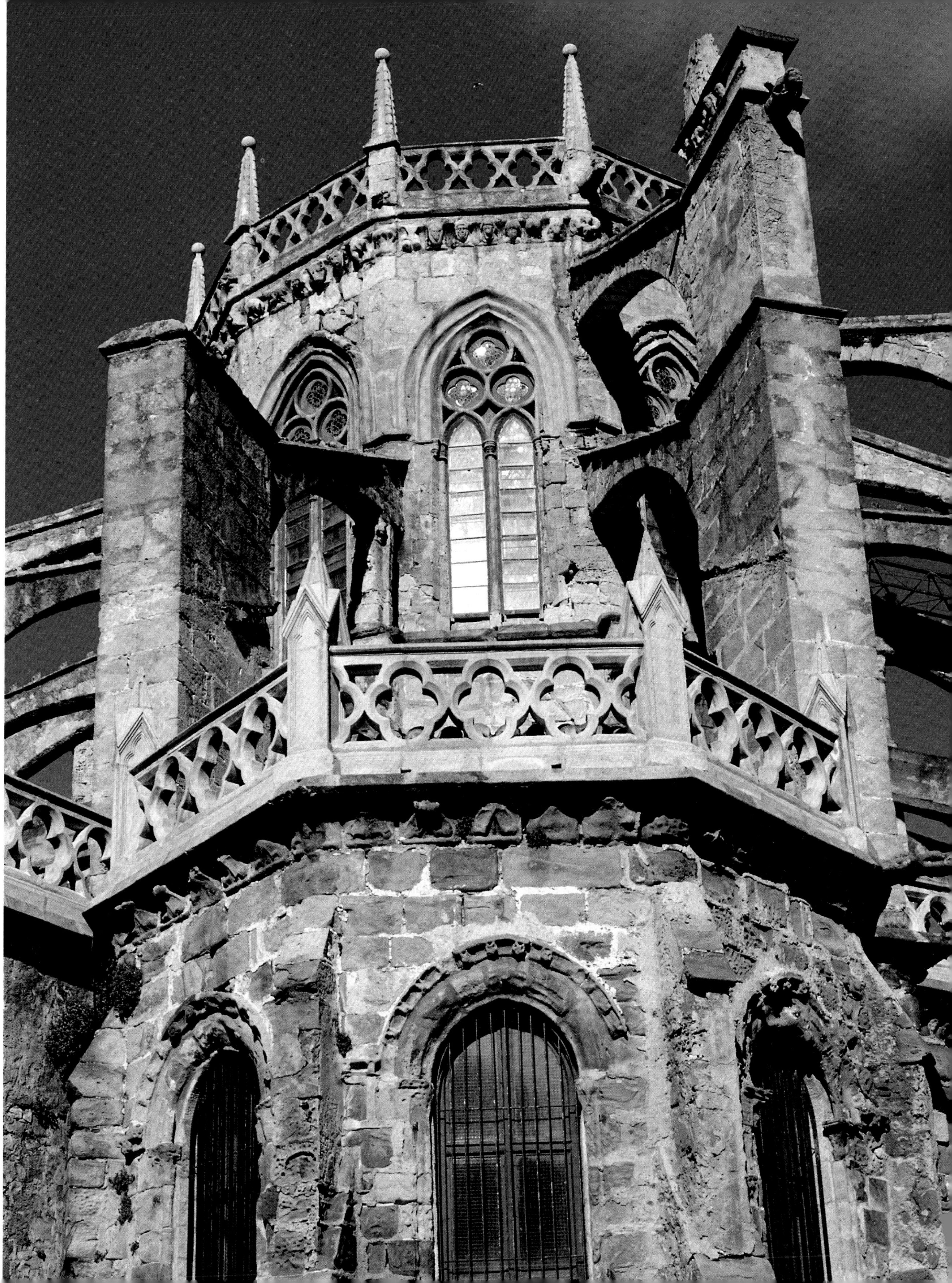

154.
Three hundred years went into the
building of Ávila cathedral, begun in
the eleventh century. Its austere
beauty is in keeping with the city and
the surrounding countryside. ▶

152.
Palma de Mallorca's cathedral, begun
in 1230 but not finished until the
seventeenth century, is famed for its
magnificent stained-glass rose
window, 36 feet in diameter, claimed
to be the largest in the world.

153.
When approaching Palma harbor
from the sea, the first thing to catch
the eye is the cathedral, standing in the
center of a great curving bay, 12 miles
in length.

153

Portugal and Italy worked alongside 50 Spanish students on the rehabilitation of the village of Umbralejo (Guadalajara), Granadilla (Cáceres) and Bubal (Huesca). For the five previous years of its existence the scheme had been confined to Spaniards. By welcoming foreign students, who are given free board and lodging, the Ministry of Education's program is likely to attract an enthusiastic work force.

RELIGION, FIESTAS AND THE BULL RING

Not surprinsingly, given the number of institutions that indicate its presence, the Catholic Church has been a vital force in Spain for a very long time. The Reconquest from the Moors was undertaken in the name of the Church, as was the colonisation of the New World. In 1936 the cause of the Nationalists was sanctified by the Spanish Primate, a cause which led to the death of more than 4000 parish priests.

Following General Franco's victory, the Church was given increased authority, controling education and censoring films, print and the media generally. Divorce could no longer be granted, adultery could be punished by imprisonment, and after a Concordat between Spain and the Vatican in 1953, other forms of religion could not worship publicly, advertise services, own property or publish books. This law was virtually repealed in 1966, though it was not until 1978 that the Constitution allowed Spaniards to worship in total freedom. Despite the fact that the great majority of the population remains nominally Catholic, attendance at Mass is declining and the increasing materialism that invariably accompanies economic growth has led to a fall in the number ordained in holy orders.

Traditionally. the Church in Spain has been on the one hand a bulwark of conservatism, on the other a timeless inspiration for pilgrimage and celebrations which blend devotion and pageantry. One religous development that indicates change in the Church and attracts international attention from time to time is *Opus Dei* (God's Work). Approved by the Holy See in June 1950, *Opus Dei* brings together Catholics of the extreme right who belong to three categories. First in importance are the Numeraries, who live in buildings belonging to the organisation and take monastic vows of poverty, chastity and obedience. Next are the Supernumeraries, who live normal lives, keeping their membership secret, and finally there are the Associates, who undertake menial tasks.

Founded in 1928, *Opus Dei* became very powerful in the 1960s and undoubtedly provided many of the talented technocrats who helped Spains's economy grow so fast at that time. The image was blemished by the discovery that a Barcelona textile firm, MATESA, run by a member of the organisation, had improperly used government credits worth millions of dollars. It was a major scandal and Franco sacked five of his ministers, three of them members of *Opus Dei*. In 1982 Pope John Paul II granted the status of personal prelature, so that members are no longer bound by local church rules and have limited independence from them. Otherwise, the society, devoted to conservative orthodoxy, plays a lessening role, which seems inevitable given the social changes taking place.

The Church's rigid insistence on the prohibition of other faiths retrieved Spain from Islam. After the Reconquest, it was the most unifying body in the country and often, in the absence of good government or accomplished national leadership, exerted a formidable power over the lives of every Spaniard. Today, the Catholic Church is mentioned in the Constitution, but only in passing. A number of factors — dependence upon an annual grant from government, the rising cost of maintaining church property, the fact that only four out of 33 universities are owned by the Church — all suggest a contraction of influence and the likelihood that the spirit of the saints, mystics, hermits, evangelists, warrior-monks and prelates of the past will be found in the accountants, salesmen, managers, engineers and academics of the future. It used to be said "Poor Spain, so near to God, so far from Europe!" — a saying rapidly losing currency.

* * * * *

FIESTAS are the emotional safety valves of Spain. Every town has at least one, and while some are more spectacular than others. virtually all have the enticing ingredients of music, dancing, good food, wine and fireworks. The smaller village fiestas usually feature *romerías* (pilgrimages) to a venerated shrine. Everyone joins in, dressing up in local costume or their finest clothes, and some will ride on horseback. At some stage there will be a picnic and chance for the young to show off and the older villagers to criticize and reminisce.

Fiestas in Castile are more restrained, perhaps, than those further south, and likely to have more religious significance. Even so, bulls are run through the streets of Soria in June. Holy Week in Valladolid, though, is the acme of sedate religious observance. For the week before Easter the normal routines of many cities will be interrupted as celebrants commemorate the passion and death of Christ; nowhere more than in Seville, where the pageantry is extraordinarily elaborate. 'Fiesta' means 'feast' in the religious sense, but just as holy day has become holiday in English, so fiesta has acquired a broader connotation, covering all kinds of festivities. Though most pay tribute to a saint or miraculous event, they may also celebrate the harvest or vintage, the arrival of Spring, return of fishermen or a success in battle. There are ten national holidays which have fixed dates. though some autonomous provinces substitute their own:

January 1	Circumcision
January 6	Epiphany
March 19	Saint Joseph and Spanish Father's Day
May 1	Labor Day (the feast of St. Peter the Worker)
July 25	St. James, patron saint of Spain
August 15	Assumption of the Virgin Mary
October 12	National Day. Anniversary of the discovery of the New World
November 1	All Saints
December 8	Immaculate Conception
December 25	Christmas Day

In addition there are four feasts which vary according to the Church Calendar: Maundy Thursday, Good Friday, Easter Monday and Corpus Christi.

The following list of some of the best-known local festivities, given in alphabetical order, includes only a fraction of the thousands which take place each year.

Gustave Doré: illustration of Cervantes' 'Don Quixote de la Mancha'.

Calendar of Fiestas

Alcoy (Alicante)	Battles between Moors and Christians	April
Alicante	St. John's Day	June
Burgos	International Folklore Festival	June-July
Cadiz	Choir Festival and Carnival	February
Evissa (Ibiza)	Fiesta. Battle of Flowers	August
Jerez de la Frontera	Spring Fair	May
Lloret de Mar	Fiesta	July
Logroño (La Rioja)	Wine Festival	September
Madrid	San Isidoro (patron saint)	May
Pamplona	Running the bulls	July
Ronda	Bullfight; historical origins celebrated	September
Salamanca	Virgin's Birthday	September
San Sebastian	La Semana Grande (Big Week)	August
Santiago de Compostella	Celebration for national saint	July
Seville	Holy Week	Before Easter
	La Feria (Fair)	April
Valdepeñas	Wine Festival	September
Valencia	Las Fallas (Carnival)	March
Vitoria (Basque)	Festival of the White Virgin	August

BULLFIGHTING (*corrida de toros*) is often part of a fiesta, or can be, as on the occasion of the running of the bulls in Pamplona, the central attraction. There are over 350 bull rings in Spain; the most celebrated are probably those in Ronda, Seville, Madrid and Barcelona. The season begins on March 19 and continues until October 12, National Day. Little in the Spanish way of life is so controversial as the corrida. From the viewpoint of the *aficionado*, it combines rich pageantry with a thrilling confrontation between a man possessed of courage, skill and dignity and a bull bred for ferocity and a willingness to charge everything that moves. At the other extreme, the bullfight is seen as an unequal and brutal spectacle that has no place in a civilised community. Spaniards themselves debate whether the corrida is a cruel slaughter left over from dark corners of the past or the domination of man over beast transformed into an art. If the difficulty most foreigners experience in procuring a ticket is any yardstick, the debate has not led to a decline in popularity. The ticket problem is compounded by the fact that, outside Madrid and Barcelona, only a handful of towns stage more than ten corridas in the nine-month season.

Although the climax may not be to every watcher's taste, few remain untouched by excitement when the Grand Entry begins to the strains of the *paso-doble* at 4-4.30 or 6-6.30 pm, according to the time of year, with the splendidly attired *toreros* and their assistants. The president tosses the keys to the bull enclosure and to the sound of bugles and drums the first of the six bulls enters the ring. Usually three to five years old, it wears the colors of the ranch on which it was bred. After the first, short session to assess the character of the bull, the *picadors* appear on horseback and lance the animal between the shoulder blades to determine its courage. Next the (*bandilleras*) near the wounds left by the *picadores*. The final phase is *la suerta de la muerta*. While his assistants keep the bull preoccupied, the matador formally requests the president's permission to make the kill. Now the matador is on his own, working towards the Moment of Truth, leading the animal with deft passes of his red cape (*muleta*). The end comes, or should do, with a precise sword thrust over the horns, down between the shoulder blades to the heart, bringing instant death. But if the thrust is bungled, the conclusion can be drawn-out, to the rising derision of the crowd. When the matador has performed with great skill, the president will award an ear, or two, or even the tail as well. The bull's carcase, which may weigh half a ton, is dragged away by mules, the sand leveled, and the ring made ready for the entrance of the next animal. Usually the whole corrida, the killing of six bulls, lasts about an hour and a half. Some moments will be elegantly balletic, some reminiscent of gladiatorial combat, and some cause the onlooker to ponder about life, death, and man's domination over animals.

THE ARTS

Spain's rate of recovery from the trauma of the Civil War varied according to the severity and location of the wound. The economy picked up in the 1950s, the tourist industry in the 60s; it was the turn of democracy and the monarchy in the 70s, while general living standards rose appreciably in the 80s. The arts, however, have been slow to mend, possibly because so many artists were Republican sympathisers who went into exile.

LANGUAGE AND LITERATURE

It is a paradox that the Spanish language, an instrument which has contributed so much to Spanish unity, to its laws, institutions and the spread of empire in the New World and beyond, should also be divisive. Spanish, which is most often called Castilian (*Castellano*) by Spaniards, has an official form going back to 1230 and is spoken as a first language by around 75 percent of the population. The remainder may or may not speak fluent Spanish but prefer a regional tongue, mostly Catalan or Euskara (the Basque language).

Catalan is a Romance language related to the French spoken in parts of southern France, as well as to Spanish. Forbidden during the thirty-six year rule of General Franco, the language has experienced a remarkable resurgence. Euskara is unusual in being a living European language which does not belong to the Indo-European family. It has fascinated linguists and anthropologists alike for a century or more, though they seem to be no nearer than ever to solving the mystery of its origin. Elsewhere in Spain there are linguistic variations in Galicia, Mallorca and Valencia, as well as dialects which are highly localised and often incomprehensible to speakers of pure Castilian. It is probable that membership of the European Community and the consequent emphasis upon English, French, German and Italian will diminish the controversy over regional language, as it has elsewhere in Europe. There is, after all, a limited number of languages that can be learned except by the most gifted linguists, and Brussels is unlikely to attempt to impose uniformity of language in the manner of Madrid in the past.

Don Rodrigo Calderón, drawn before his execution in 1621, a contemporary of the famous playwright of the same name.

* * * * *

Spanish literature, despite great achievements dating back to the twelfth-century *Cantar de Mío Cid*, had rarely traveled well. Perhaps Spanish genius has flourished in so many other forms, literature has been relatively neglected. The Inquisition and church censorship may have played a part. It is also possible that in the past the solitary, self-indulgent pleasure of reading had little appeal in a gregarious, active society, or the price of books prohibited ownership. Great as the number of poets, playwrights, essayists and mystics is, across the sun-drenched plains of Spain there first falls the archetypal shadow of that most Spanish of all characters, Don Quixote.

The latter part of the sixteenth century and most of the seventeenth came to be known as the Golden Age of Spanish literature and Miguel Cervantes (1547-1616) was by far the most original writer of that period. He went to Italy in 1569, where he served in the household of a Cardinal Aquaviva and in 1570 enlisted in the army as a private. At the battle of Lepanto (1571) he was wounded and lost the use of his left arm. Returning to Spain, he was captured by the Moors and held in Algiers as a slave until ransomed by his parents in 1580. Not surprisingly after such an experience, he retired from the army and married. He wrote poems and plays without much success until in 1605, at the age of fifty-eight, the first part was published of his masterpiece, *Don Quixote de la Mancha*, the prototype of the modern novel. The second part followed in 1615, a year before his death.

Cervantes, determined, persevering, resourceful, patriotic, never prospering, has been compared to his great hero. It is a mark of the quality of Don Quixote that 'quixotic' has found a place in the English vocabulary as an attribute for the romantic idealist, the visionary or the impractical man of action, and that the Don's adventures appeal to children and adults alike. Don Quixote, sitting his horse as erect as a flagpole, tilting at windmills (another expression appropriated by the English language), pontificating to Sancho Panza and gallantly seeking the hand of Dulcinea as the mistress of his heart, may have begun as a figure of burlesque, but gradually assumed a universal identity and, with it, the certainty of classifical status.

Lope de Vega, Cervantes' younger contemporary (1562-1635), is considered the founder of Spanish drama. Astonishingly prolific, he claimed to have written 1500 plays, some 500 of which have survived, as well as countless other works. His early life was a series of escapades and in 1587 he was banished from Madrid for libel. The next year he sailed with the Spanish Armada, which may be why he was so jubilant in his epic on the death of Sir Francis Drake. His plays, written at amazing speed, some, he admitted, in twenty-four hours, are mostly comedies in verse, distinguished by wit, a sharp eye for character and powerful dramatic effects. Late in life he took holy orders, but continued to write for the stage. He was the dominant figure in the Spanish literary life of his time; a national institution, mourned by the whole country when he died. It is Cervantes, however, who holds the higher place in world literature.

Ortega y Gasset (1883-1955) an essayist and philosopher who was appointed professor of metaphysics at Madrid University in 1910, became internationally known when his *Revolt of the Masses* was published and translated in 1932. He supported the Republic but fled the country in 1936, returning only in 1949. As early as 1929 he argued for a United States of Europe. Despite his intellectual aloofness — he argues always for the leadership of the intellectual minority without which the masses will collapse into chaos — his personal example is a poignant reminder of the dilemma of the patriotic Spanish academic in the first half of this century.

In his own words, Federico García Lorca (1899-1936) posed the dilemma: "I am totally Spanish, and it would be impossible for me to live outside my geographical limits... needless to say, I do not believe in political frontiers". Born in Granada, García Lorca was an extravagantly gifted musician, artist and writer; his godfather was Manuel de Falla, and a friend was Salvador Dalí, to whom he dedicated a discriminating ode. "... I do not sing praise to your imperfect adolescent paintbrush / But applaud the firm direction of your arrows". *Blood Wedding, Yerma* and *The House of Bernarda Alba* are a trilogy of his best-known and most frequently performed plays. He was shot by Falangists when they occupied Granada.

Since 1900, Spanish writers have won the Nobel Prize no less than five times. José Echegaray (1832-1916), a dramatist, mathematician and political economist, began as an engineer who turned to politics in his old age. He wrote 64 plays, the main theme of which is the clash of moral issues, honor and duty. He was awarded the Nobel Prize in 1904. Jacinto Benavente (1866-1954), a dramatist who lived all his life in Madrid, had a flair for farce and rustic comedy that made him popular with public and critics alike and brought him the Nobel Prize in 1922. The award went to Juan Ramón Jiménez (1881-1958) in 1956 for his lyric poetry. Born in Andalucía, Jiménez left Spain in 1936, living first in

Puerto Rico, then Cuba, and finally the U.S.A. Another Andalusian, Vicente Aleixandre (b. 1898) qualified as a lawyer in Madrid before turning increasingly to poetry writing when overtaken by ill-health in the 1920s. In the followng decade he experimented with Surrealism, and won the National Prize for Literature in 1935, followed by the Nobel Prize in 1977.

The most recent Spanish Nobel laureate is Camilo Jose Cela, a writer from Galicia who taught at the University of Palma de Mallorca. His first and most popular novel is *Pascal Duarte's Family* (published 1942, translated into English 1946). Travel books, essays and poetry followed, as well as encyclopaedias of sexual information and eroticism. In 1977, Cela was asked by king Juan Carlos to serve on the drafting committee for the Constitution, to ensure the purity and accuracy of the Castilian Spanish. In 1989 the Swedish Academy recognised Cela as the most outstanding figure in the literary renewal of postwar Spain, admiring the compassion the writer shows for the helplessness of humanity.

The loyalties of Spain have so often been divisive, and rarely more so than in the vexed question of language. Inevitably linguistic and national rights have intertwined, and any central government attempts to disentangle them by upholding the former and playing down the latter have provoked continuing dissatisfaction and controversy. With the new Constitution, provision has been made for minority languages, which, it should be borne in mind, have never been so explosive an issue as in some parts of Europe. Given the unquestionable genius of Spain and the numbers who have Spanish as a mother tongue, it is somewhat surprising that more writers have not established international reputations. In the second half of the twentieth century the most powerful and original writing in Spanish has come from Latin America, from the pens of such as Neruda, Borges, Llosa and Marquez.

MUSIC

Soul music existed in Spain long before the expression gained currency for something quite different in contemporary America. Flamenco is the soul of Spanish music. A listener needs to know little about flamenco or music to fall under the spell of a guitarist displaying dazzling virtuosity, strumming chords punctuated by thrilling changes of rhythm. And when the singer joins him in a primitive, ecstatic dialogue, the two artists set every heart pounding in time with the harsh, throbbing music. It is intoxicating, improvised, and very closely associated with the gypsies, who have maintained a splendid earthiness in their emotion-charged singing and passionate dancing. It is said that 'flamenco' was a pejorative term given to the boisterous Flemings at the court of Charles V in 1517. The music may have origins in Arabic, Jewish and Byzantine themes, while the dancing may be the contribution of gypsy refugees from India. Gypsies have certainly established themselves as custodians of the music, which they have passed down for generations among families, villages and districts, always improvising, yet keeping alive that essential violence, truth and simplicity.

Flamenco is by no means the only form of popular musical expression. Each region has its own distinctive folk music. Galician rhythms and bagpipes, for instance, are strongly reminiscent of Scottish and Irish folk music, testifying to common Celtic origins.

Music in the more classical tradition did not have a great many distinguished composers or artists who attracted international attention until the late nineteenth century. Pablo Sarasate (1844-1908), born in Pamplona, studied violin and composition at the Paris Conservatoire, where he won first prize. A brilliant London debut in 1861 led to concerts all over the world. Saint-Saëns composed both his first and third violin concertos with his sweet tone and classical style in mind.

Isaac Albeniz (1860-1909) was an infant prodigy who first performed in Barcelona when four years of age. He studied piano in Paris when seven and was tutored by Liszt, who helped him perfect his technique. From the age of twenty onwards he devoted himself increasingly to composition, his famous Iberian Suite coming just before his death from Bright's disease in France.

Enrique Granados (1867-1916) was a brilliant pianist who studied in Paris and later composed operas, suites, symphonic poems and a range of pieces for the piano. Returning to Europe in 1916, after the triumphant première of his opera *Goyescas* at the New York Metropolitan, he was drowned together with his wife when the liner *Sussex* in which they were traveling was torpedoed in the English Channel by a German U-boat.

Pablo Casals (1876-1973), the great Catalan cellist, who was also a conductor, composer and pianist, gained royal patronage through Ibeniz and won a scholarship to Brussels in 1895. He performed for Queen Victoria in 1899, and after his first U.S. tour in 1901 was launched as the world's foremost cellist. In protest against the Franco regime he moved to Prades, a Catalan-speaking village in France, vowing never to return while Spain had a totalitarian government. In 1956 he settled in Puerto Rico, but continued to perform all over the world until well past the age of ninety.

Also born in 1876 (in Cadiz) was Manual de Falla. If not the most gifted Spanish composer of all time, he is certainly the best known abroad. After studying and teaching, he followed the familiar path to Paris in 1907, and became a friend of Ravel and Debussy. The ballet-pantomime *El Amor Brujo* was first performed in 1915, and the next year de Falla published *Nights in the Gardens of Spain*, to be followed in 1919 by Diaghilev's production of *The Three-Cornered Hat*, a ballet that took London by storm. In the same year de Falla dedicated *Fantasia Baetica* to Arthur Rubenstein (*Baetica* was the Roman name for Andalucía). He moved to Argentina in 1936, and died there in 1946. José Iturbí, a Valencian pianist and conductor who settled in the United States, brought prominence to de Falla by his acclaimed performances of *Ritual Fire Dance*.

Undoubtedly the most popular Spanish composer of more recent times has been Joaquin Rodrigo (born 1901), blind from the age of three, who after studying in Paris became professor of music at the University of Madrid in 1946. His concerto for guitar, *Concierto de Aranjuez* (1939) was performed all over the world in the 1960s and 70s.

Two very different performers: Placido Domingo, a thrilling lyrical and heroic tenor, and Julio Iglesias, a polished performer of Latin popular songs, are the Spanish voices most often heard throughout the world today.

159.
A traditional dance performed in
Tarragona. The fiesta has helped to
keep alive folk music and regional
dress, which have virtually
disappeared in many western
countries.

157

157.
An open-air 'new' mass on the feast of
Our Lady of Ujué (Navarre).

158.
Holy Week in Cuenca is celebrated
with all the fervor of the South.

158

160.
Santillana del Mar is not, as its name suggests, by the sea, but some miles inland. Its closeness to the Altamira Caves and its picturesque old buildings have made it a popular stop for tourists in northern Spain.

161.
A square in the town of Pontevedra on the west coast of Galicia. Most of its ancient buildings are constructed of granite.

163.
The Casa de los Picos in Segovia takes its name from its unusual façade studded with stones which was added to this fourteent-century fortified dwelling in about 1500.

162.
A cemetery in Madrid. The closeness of family ties is reflected in the care lavished on the upkeep of graves.

164.
A Benedictine abbey was founded at San Millán de la Cogolla (Logroño) in the sixth century and rebuilt in such grand style in the sixteenth that it gained the name 'the Escorial of La Rioja'. ▶

165.
The Ebro at Lodosa (Navarre). Known as the Iberus in ancient times, it is the only one of the five great rivers of the Iberian peninsula to empty into the Mediterranean. From Cantabria it flows for 576 miles, gathering 222 tributaries, before reaching its delta in the Tarragona region. ▶▶

166.
Alone of all creatures man possesses the use of fire, a subject of cult veneration from earliest times. Here, fire is the centerpiece of the fiesta of San Juan in Guipúzcoa, the heart of the Basque lands. ▶▶▶

167.
The Mediterranean coast attracts
more tourists than Santander's
Biscayan beaches, but there are many
who prefer its fresher climate and less
crowded and commercialised
coastline.

167

168.
These gay beach-huts
near La Coruña
retain an old-
fashioned appeal,
reminiscent of the
days when sea-
bathing was a more
discreet affair.

168

169.
San Sebastian: a shore of briny, seaweed smells, Atlantic rollers crashing onto the sands and striped poles, a marine match for the windmills of La Mancha.

169

170.
On the island of Mallorca (Majorca), the largest of the Balearics, fishing has been replaced by tourism as the major source of income.

170

174.
A potter at work in Jaén, an area famous for handcrafts. Spain's major contribution to pottery is majolica ware, the name coming from Mallorca (Majorca). In the thirteenth century Valencians pioneered the technique of firing the clay object, coating it with a tin glaze, refiring, then decorating it in brilliant colors before the final firing. ▸

173.
A fairground in Bilbao (Ibaizábel in the Basque language), a thriving industrial city and river port of half a million inhabitants. Its iron and steel industry relies on the rich iron (hematite) mines nearby.

176.
Blood and sand, man and beast, grace and brutality — the corrida is hard to beat for drama and sheer spectacle, as here at the Plaza de las Ventas in Madrid. ▸▸▸

175.
The bullring in Málaga, a city founded by the Phoencians and later occupied by the Moors for almost 800 years. Now the thriving metropolitan center of the Costa del Sol, Málaga's population of more than half a million ensures that every seat at the corrida will be occupied. ▸▸

171.
Spain has remained relatively 'uncorrupted' by fast-food outlets, apart from the areas catering heavily to foreign tourists. A leisurely meal of authentic Spanish food is offered by 'tabernas' like this one in Madrid.

172.
Sherry is made only in the province of Cadiz, primarily in the area near the town of Jerez de la Frontera. British mispronunciation led to the abbreviation 'Sherry'. The British drink some two-thirds of all Spanish exports of this wine, and even make their own version.

172

179.
The lonely contest of man and bull
enacted in a thronged, but hushed
arena on a hot afternoon.

177.
Matadors wear the distinctive
glittering 'trajes de luces' or suits of
lights. Clipped to the back of the head,
just beneath the black hat, the
'montera', is the pigtail, the trademark
of the bullfighter.

177

178

178.
Garish posters fantasise the
proceedings in the bullring and offer
scope for further fantasy: for an
additional payment, the purchaser's
own name can be substituted for that
of a renowned 'matador de toros'.

180.
The grand entry into the bullring in
Seville. The nearby tobacco factory is
a part of operatic history as the place
where Carmen earned her living.

181.
As a display of male dominance, the bullfight would be pointless without admiring females, like these Andalusian lovelies in a carriage.

182

182.
Some siestas are more comfortable than others. Here a driver catnaps in his carriage.

183.
Where there are churches there are belfries, bells and views across roofs, as here at Carmona, a town near Seville, on a summer afternoon of sun-drenched silence.

186.
Seville, capital of the fiesta, also celebrates a Holy Week more starkly dramatic than any in Europe. ▶

187.
The very name of Seville is suggestive of gaiety, song and romance. But the city has a more serious side, as this scene in Holy Week suggests. ▶▶

184

184.
The region of Seville, Spain's major inland port, has been open to a miscellany of influences. Here, on the façade of the Palacio de la Gomera in Osuna, the severe windows contrast with the elaborate doorway.

185

185.
A wrought-iron ornamental sunburst above a gateway to a patio in Seville. The patio is an essential element in the life style of Andalucía.

187

188.
Dressed in their traditional best, this couple brighten the local scene.

189.
Covadonga, scene of a famous, though in fact rather small, battle, in which the Visigoth leader Pelayo and 300 warriors ambushed and defeated Moorish forces in 718, checking their advance into Asturias.

190.
The core of Spain is a tableland of ancient rocks, parched in summer and swept by icy winds in winter. Although majestically beautiful, millions of acres are partially or totally unproductive. ▶

191.
The southern, Spanish slopes of the Pyrenees are mostly gentler than the steeper, French side. In an area of great scenic beauty lies the Ordesa National Park, seen with the sheer escarpment of Mount Perdido. ▶▶

194.
Emperor Trajan (A.D. 57-117), a native of Spain and the first non-Italian to wear the purple, is said to have built a lighthouse here on the coast of La Coruña, Galicia. ▶

192.
The Coto Doñana, 60 miles southwest of Seville, is perhaps the largest roadless area in Western Europe. Along the straight, sandy shore stand stone towers, built to ward off Barbary pirates, where peregrines now breed. Inland grow stone pine and cork oak, harboring storks and herons. Lagoons provide a habitat for spectacular flamingoes.

195.
The Alhambra, Granada, arguably one of the most beautiful fortified palaces ever fashioned by man, is incontestably the finest example of Moorish architecture in Spain. ▶▶

196.
The great honeycomb dome with over 5000 cells in the Hall of the Two Sisters (Sala de las Dos Hermanes), which may have been part of the harem of the Alhambra palace. ▶▶▶

193

193.
Punta de la Arena on the Basque coast. Not far inland lies the little town of Guernica, ruthlessly bombed in the Civil War, an act which inspired one of Picasso's most famous paintings.

199.
An intricate stalactite arch in the
Court of the Lions of the Alhambra
palace.

197.
Part of the intricate decoration of the
Court of the Lions (Patio de los
Leones) in the Alhambra. The absence
of figural ornamentation in Muslim
art is compensated by the elegant
calligraphy of religious inscriptions.

198.
Typical Moorish tiles
in the Alcázar,
Toledo.

198

200.
Every inch of the internal wall space
of the Alhambra is covered with lavish
decoration in stone, wood, stucco and
ceramics. Most of the palace was built
and ornamented in the fourteenth
century.

202.
The Court of the Lions: 124 marble
columns, 11 feet high, support the
graceful arcading of stilted arches
surrounding the fountain with 12
lions. The court was begun in 1377,
during the reign of Sultan
Mohammed V.

200

201.
A dazzling array of
multifaceted designs
in the stucco
decoration above
windows in the Hall
of the Two Sisters in
the Alhambra.

201

203.
The Generalife Garden, dating from the early fourteenth century, belonged to the summer palace of the sultans, overlooking the Alhambra palace in Granada.

204

203

204.
The Court of Myrtles of the Alhambra, commissioned by Sultan Yussuf I (1334-1354), is the only classical Islamic garden to have survived intact in Spain.

205.
The Torre de las Damas, one of the many towers of the Alhambra, with a typically Moorish blend of water, vegetation and graceful arches.

205

206

206.
The Court of Myrtles (Patio de los Arrayanes) can easily be peopled, in the mind's eye, with gowned and turbaned figures deep in religious meditation or diplomatic conversation.

209.
The graceful colonnades of the interior of the Alhambra epitomise the serene, yet intricate beauty of Moorish architecture. ▶

207.
The Hall of the Ambassadors (Salon de Embajadores), the largest room in the Alhambra, and one of the most exquisitely decorated, occupies two storeys in the Torre de Comares.

208.
As its name suggests, it was in the Hall of the Ambassadors that the enthroned sultans gave audience to foreign emissaries, who could scarcely fail to be impressed by its opulent beauty.

ARCHITECTURE AND PAINTING

Art in Spain goes sublimely back to the Altamira cave paintings. The earliest monuments, however, date from the Roman occupation, though there are some traces of Iberian and Greek settlements. Many towns have remains of Roman reservoirs, triumphal arches and columns, while the aqueduct at Segovia and bridge at Alcantara are oustanding examples of Roman engineering genius. Mérida, Tarragona and Córdoba also have substantial remains testifying to the designing and building skills of the empire between the third century B.C. and fifth century A.D. Later, from the ninth century onward, the Moors left monuments to their architectural virtuosity — mosques, palces, fortifications — chiefly in Seville, Córdoba and Granada, adding refinements in ceramics, carving and metalwork to grand architectural design.

Although there have been a variety of parallel and overlapping lines of development in Spanish art, inspiration and execution most often looked to France or Rome for their stimulus. As a rule, artists responded to French technique, while their themes were indebted to commissions from the Church or the court. The international styles of architecture, beginning with Early Christian art and moving through Romanesque, Gothic, Renaissance and Baroque, all bear the imprint of Spanish genius, sometimes with a pronounced Moorish influence. They have left behind the most visible portion of Spain's rich artistic patrimony: cathedrals, castles, convents, palaces, and whole walled cities.

The same styles traveled well when transposed to Spain's colonies from the sixteenth to nineteenth centuries. In Peru and Mexico, where skilled craftsmen familiar with monumental building were to be found, the progress and development of Spanish architecture was later matched in the colonies. The earliest cathedral in America is Santo Domingo (1521-1541), which had immediately recognisable hallmarks of the grand Spanish style. The Augustinian, Franciscan and Dominican orders in Mexico were outstanding builders. They introduced an open chapel for the Indians with walls on only three sides, which was not only cooler but quicker to build and accommodated more people. In Spanish colonial domestic architecture the use of balconies — where occupants often slept on hot nights — was a replica of the Andalusian style, and subsequently copied in many other tropical and semi-tropical countries.

* * * * *

The first notable painter to capture the harshness and melancholy that distinguishes much of Spanish art was Luis de Morales (1509-1586), who lived and painted in Bajadoz, his birthplace. His sharply etched portrayals of saintly suffering were very popular and much imitated. However, an invitation to paint for the Escorial produced work that did not meet with the approval of Philip II, and Morales returned home. Fine examples of his work hang in the Prado.

El Greco (1541-1614), an adopted Spaniard, was born Domenicos Theotocopoulos in Crete, then in the possession of Venice, where he went at the age of nineteen to study under Titian. He moved to Madrid to seek work at the Escorial, but the king did not care for the radiance of his color, so El Greco settled in Toledo where, after 1590, his output was enormous. He signed his paintings in full, in Greek. His attenuated figures and vibrant hues were not as much appreciated as his dynamic expressions of religious ecstasy, and he was less patronised than his original talent would seem to demand. As he grew older, El Greco accentuated his own stylistic features. He influenced Velázquez, who was an admirer of his work, and his ascetic faces are to be found in the work of Spanish artists of later times. He was buried in Toledo, but all trace of his grave was lost when the church housing the family vault was destroyed.

José de Ribera (1590-1652) studied in Valencia before moving to Naples (a Spanish possession at the time) where, under the nickname of *Lo Spagnoletto*, he painted mostly religious and classical works at the court of the Spanish viceroy, many of which were sent back to Spain as gifts. His life was as dramatic as his Mannerist paintings, and despite great popularity and prosperity along the way, he died in poverty in Naples.

Diego Velázquez (1599-1660), the most celebrated of the Spanish Old Masters, was born in Seville, where his outstanding gifts were sufficiently recognised for him to move to Madrid in 1622, under the patronage of the Count of Olivares. In 1624 he was elevated to the post of court painter, and over the years formed a strong friendship with Philip IV. Velázquez made two significant visits to Italy. The first, in 1629, enabled him to see, and be influenced by, the works of some of the leading Italian, especially Venetian, painters; the second was a commission by Philip IV to buy paintings to grace the royal collection, many of which now hang in the Prado. His own production, although helped by assistants, is not large — no more perhaps than a hundred or so authentically autographed paintings are known, most of them in Madrid. His stature as an artist became recognised fully only in the nineteenth century, when his works, and the replicas he was obliged to provide, were shown outside the confines of the royal court.

Another outstanding Baroque artist from Seville is Velázquez' contemporary, Francisco Zurbarán (1598-1664), one of Spain's foremost painters of religious subjects.

Francisco Goya (1746-1828) studied in Zaragoza, where he was born, and later moved to Madrid, then to Rome, and back to Madrid, where he married in 1775. His early works convey the freedom and charm of popular life, but after his appointment as painter to the court, where he was a great favorite, he became increasingly somber. His etchings of the disasters of war, witches and monsters were the reactions of a sensitive man appalled by the events of his time. He went deaf at sixty, after which his work becomes steadily more melancholic. His extraordinary candor in some royal portraits, where he employs exquisite technique to depict a family that, although they supported him, he clearly despised, has few parallels in commissioned art. He was given permission to depart for France in 1824 and died in Bordeaux at the age of eighty-two. Few artists have composed such a variety of work. Although well represented in many American and European galleries, the bulk and diversity of his output is best seen, like that of Velázquez, in Madrid.

In the twentieth century three very different, major artists have re-established Spanish eminence in a more publicised manner than their predecessors. Pablo Picasso (1881-1973), born the son of an artist in Málaga, studied in Barcelona and established himself in Paris in 1900, where he soon became associated with leading innovators of his time, such as Derain, Braque and Matisse. A creator of Cubism, together with his fellow-countryman Juan Gris (1887-1927), he went through a dazzling variety of abstract styles, summed up in his own words: "Through art we express our conception of what nature is not". His *Guernica* echoes Goya's abhorrence of war, though his versatility and tireless invention are uniquely his own.

Salvador Dalí (1904-1989) tried Cubism, but deserted abstract art to win fame as an eccentric Surrealist painter of immediately recognisable, exceptional draftsmanship. A cosmopolitan who emigrated to the U.S.A. in 1940, Dalí returned to settle on the Costa Brava, where the Dalí Museum contains an extraordinary collection of inventive and whimsical fantasies.

Another, very different, Catalan Surrealist, Joan Miró (1895-1983), used brilliant pure color and abstract forms to express himself, forms which decorate the walls of the UNESCO headquarters in Paris and can be seen, perhaps at their best, in the Fundacio Miró, the lovely, pure white, cultural center in Barcelona. His poster for the 1982 World Cup is an example of commissioned Spanish art moving significantly from depicting the saints to soccer.

The majority of the masterpieces of Spanish art, until relatively recently, were largely commissioned by the Church, the court and grandees. French and Italian artistic influences were strong in Spain, as elsewhere in Europe. Other influential factors were the pilgrimage and trade routes, the Moorish occupation, and possessions in the Lowlands and Italy. Spanish artists of earlier centuries, for their part, had little impact elsewhere in Europe. The religious themes, aquiline faces, carefulness and general absence of optimism were neither readily accesible to other European artists nor likely to "enlarge the human mind and pull mankind a few steps up the hill..." — in the dismissive words of art critic Sir Kenneth Clark.

One recent development gives encouragement for a view that Spanish art, like so many other aspects of the country, may be due for re-evaluation. In the mide-1980s the Spanish government amended tax legislation concerning the ownership of works of art, whereupon thousands of paintings came to light. Some may raise the vexed questions of attestation of authorship, the work of pupils and the production of copies. Whatever the problems, any thoughtful judgement on the place of Spanish art is likely to take a little longer as a result.

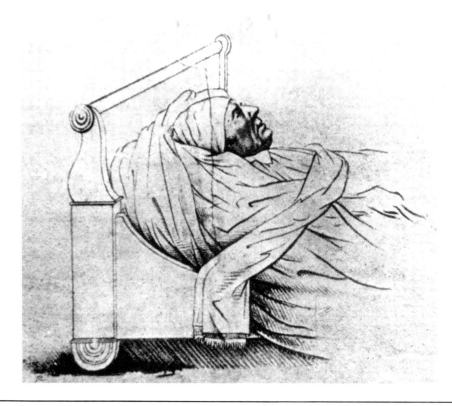

Goya drawn on his deathbed (April 16, 1828) by F. de la Torre.

Major Historical Events

Charles I of Spain, better known as Emperor Charles V of the Holy Roman Empire.

15,000 B.C.   Cro-Magnon man dwells in caves near Santillana del Mar (Santander province) and illustrates his hunt for food on the walls of the Altamira Caves.

3000 B.C.   Iberians, an African people, settle in the south then, spread east as far as the Pyrenees.

1000 B.C.   Phoenicians establish trading centers, notably Gadir (Cadiz), on the Atlantic seaboard.

800-700 B.C.   Bands of Celts cross the Pyrenees to settle among the Iberians.

600-500 B.C.   Phoenician settlements absorbed by Carthage, its ex-colony, a growing Mediterranean power. Greeks establish enclaves on the east coast.

220-200 B.C.   The Punic Wars, Rome versus Carthage, involve Spain. Hannibal's defeat by Scipio in North Africa ends Carthaginian influence.

200 B.C.-A.D. 400   Iberian Peninsula divided into Roman provinces. Rapid development and exploitation in the first two centuries A.D.

409   First waves of Vandals and other barbarians corss the Pyrenees but do not settle.

414   Visigoths arrive, settle, establish Toledo as the capital and their leader as king.

589   Visigoth King Reccared renounces Arianism and converts to Roman Catholicism, which becomes the state religion.

711   The Berber Tariq invades Spain and conquers the peninsula in seven years.

718   Pelayo, the Visigoth leader, begins the Reconquest with victory at Covadonga.

732   Arabs (Moors) defeated at Poitiers by Charles Martel. They settle south of the Pyrenees.

929-1031   Abd-ar-Rahman founds the Córdoba caliphate.

1000-1033   Navarre leads resistante to Moors.

1086   Almoravides from North Africa reinforce Moors.

1099   El Cid dies in Valencia.

1151   Almohades replace Almoravides and conquer Almería.

1217-1252   Ferdinand III of Castile captures Córdoba and Seville. Only Granada remains to the Moors.

1469   Ferdinand and Isabella marry, and unite Aragón and Castile (1479).

1480   Inquisition established to investigate loyalty of Jews, marking the beginning of three centuries of religious persecution.

1492   Muslim Granada falls to Christians. Columbus discovers the New World. Jews expelled.

1516-1556   Charles I, ruler of the Netherlands, becomes Charles V, first Hapsburg king of Spain and Holy Roman Emperor.

1519-1521   Hernán Cortés lands in Mexico and by taking the Aztec capital, Tenochitlan, secures Mexico for Spain.

1531   Francisco Pizarro conquers Peru.

1530-1580   Period of exploration and colonisation of the New World.

1561 Philip II (succeeded Charles V in 1556) moves his capital to Madrid and begins building the Escorial.

1568-1648 Protestant Netherlands revolts, start of an eighty-year war leading to Dutch independence.

1571 Battle of Lepanto: Muslim sea-power is crushed by combined fleets of Spain, Venice and Papal States, commanded by Don John of Austria.

1588 The Great Armada, sent to chastise Protestant England, is defeated.

1609 Expulsion of about 300,000 Moriscos (Christianised Muslims).

1621-1700 Spain fights fruitless wars with English, French, Turks and Dutch.

1640 Catalonia revolts and Portugal seizes independence.

1700 Charles II dies; Philip IV, a Bourbon, succeeds him.

1702-1714 War of Spanish Succession. Austria acquires most of Spain's European possessions.

1767 Charles III orders expulsion of Jesuits.

1793-1805 France invades Spain and forces an alliance. The Combined Fleets of France and Spain are defeated at Trafalgar.

1808-1814 Napoleon makes his brother, Joseph, king of Spain. Wellington supports Spanish guerillas against French occupiers.

1821 Venezuela becomes independent, followed by other South American colonies.

1833-1839 First Carlist War.

1875-1885 Restoration of monarchy after a brief republic. Reign of Alphonso XII.

1898 Spanish-American War. Spain loses Puerto Rico, Cuba and Philippines.

1923-1930 Dictatorship of Primo de Rivera.

1931 Alphonso XIII leaves the country; a republic declared.

1923-1936 A government of the Right.

1936 Coalition of left-wing parties wins election.

1936-1939 Right-wing generals lead a coup that results in civil war. General Francisco Franco emerges as the leader.

1939-1945 Franco keeps Spain neutral yet sympathetic to the Axis.

1945-1953 Spain an outcast from all major political groups and U.N. In 1953, U.S.A. provides aid in return for military bases.

1955 Spain joins United Nations.

1959 ETA Basque terrorist group established.

1969 Juan Carlos de Bourbon declared Franco's successor.

1975 Juan Carlos crowned.

1981 Attempted military coup, in which Colonel Tejero threatens parliament.

1982 Spain becomes sixteenth member of NATO. Spanish Socialists, led by Felipe Gonzáles, win national elections overwhelmingly.

1986 Spain joins the European Common Market.

1989 Gonzáles re-elected.

1992 Madrid: European capital of culture. Barcelona: venue of Summer Olympics. Seville: World's Fair and celebration of five-hundredth anniversary of Columbus' voyage.

Queen Isabella, whose marriage to King Ferdinand resulted in a united Spain.

Index

Gustave Doré: illustration of Cervantes' 'Don Quixote de la Mancha'.

LA CORUÑ

O

SEVIL

ISLAS CANARIAS

LA PALMA
TENERIFE